To Harriet

There's no such word as can't!

Good Luck!

Tim Stubbs

TIM STOCKDALE

There's no such word as can't!

TIM STOCKDALE

First published in Great Britain in 2012 by
Tim Stockdale

The right of Tim Stockdale to be identified as the
author of this work has been asserted in
accordance with the Copyright, Designs and
Patents Act 1988.

A catalogue record for this book is available from
The British Library.

HARDBACK ISBN 978-0-9574750-0-7

Set in 12.25/14.75pt Baskerville
Printed in Great Britain by CPI Group (UK)
Croydon, Surrey CR0 4YY

Photographs: Bob Atkins/Horse&Rider magazine,
Anthony Reynolds, Trevor Meeks,
Catch It Quick Photography

This book is dedicated to my wonderful family. First, to my darling wife, Laura, for her unwavering support and selfless attitude. And also to my two sons, Joseph and Mark. I just get prouder of you every day.

Contents

Contents

Contents continued

Foreword

There is no other sport that can capture the emotion of winning more than showjumping, particularly at a major indoor show. When the curtain opens into the main arena and from the blacked-out stadium, the spotlight shines on the victor. The crowd goes wild. The proud beauty and majesty of the horse, the happiness and joy of the rider in their immaculate breeches and sharp jacket, clothing that's such a chore on a really hot day, but under those conditions, looks perfect. And for one brief moment, the riders can enjoy their win and put to the back of their minds the slog, the heartache and the sacrifices they've had to make to put themselves in this adulated scene.

There have been many riders who have achieved this over the years, but in the history of showjumping, it is only a small number who have had the ability, tenacity and willpower to keep achieving at the highest level, to be on Championship and Olympic teams. One of those is Tim Stockdale.

The fact that Tim didn't come from a horsey background makes his story all the more remarkable. He just learnt as he went along, and on that long journey, he has attributed some of those character-forming years to the period he spent on my yard in the early Eighties.

Tim has reminded me recently of our first meeting when he came for an interview when I was based in Thirsk, North Yorkshire. Apparently I said: "I'm short of time and have to go to Harrogate, so jump in the car and we'll talk as we go along."

He remembered that on reaching Harrogate, I couldn't find a place to park, so I parked on a double yellow line. I said I'd only be 30 minutes, at which stage he nervously pointed out that it was illegal to park where I was. "Don't worry," I said, "just open up the bonnet and pretend you're fixing the engine!"

Tim later recounted: "I was almost peeing my pants for each of those 30 nervous minutes!"

He wondered what sort of lunatic he'd come to work for and although we would never repeat those sort of antics, Tim came to realise that ours was a profession where you had to think on your feet. Crucially, for instance, that the time in the arena to show your talents was a small part compared to finding horses. Which ones are capable of jumping at the highest level, which ones want selling, how to find owners and keep their interest, how to keep the day-to-day running of a yard efficient and yet still have time for a laugh and a joke.

Tim had the ability and the hard-working ethos to have made it without me, but if in some small way I have contributed to the popular showjumping rider that Tim Stockdale has become today, then it makes me very proud to be part of this remarkable story.

Graham Fletcher

Chapter 1

It wasn't supposed to end like this

- A time for reflection
- Would I walk again?
- My irrational fear
- Was this the end?

Was it going to be all over… this career that had given me years of fun, taken me around the world on some of the best horses I've been fortunate enough to ride? And with some of the nicest and most generous owners and sponsors I've been lucky enough to call my friends. It wasn't supposed to end with me broken, on the floor of a cold arena in deepest Wales. This career that has seen me win the Longines King George V Gold Cup at Hickstead in 2010, the trophy I'd set my heart on since I saw Mike Saywell scoop that glittering prize on Chainbridge 35 years earlier.

As a showjumper, you don't go into this sport thinking you're never going to get hurt – in fact, no one should ever get on a horse if they're worried about falling off. It all goes with the territory. Horses are unpredictable animals, as I discovered that day in October 2011, the 17th to be precise. Of course, you do everything in your power to prevent the knocks and bumps and bruises, but this was a big one – a major fall, one I bank on getting every four years or so, interspersed with the odd collarbone fracture or cracked rib thrown in for good measure along the way. The last serious prang was when Ruby (Fresh Direct Corlato) misjudged the small board in front of a water jump in a competition in Portugal in 2006, which resulted in me smashing into the floor once again. Then I'd bust some ribs. And now, here was my time again.

Would I have to rethink my life completely or would I still be able to pursue the career that my beautiful, long-suffering wife, Laura, had supported me through, enjoying the highs and managing the lows. Laura is my rock. I couldn't do it without her – or my beloved sons, Joseph and Mark, both chips off the old block with their love of riding horses and playing cricket.

But was my time going to be up, once and for all? I suppose up to this point I'd been pretty lucky, and serious neck injuries are not uncommon in my sport.

Although I am leading what some call a glamorous lifestyle and one that many would give their eye teeth for, I don't enjoy the travelling and being away from my family to do my job. For me, the best part of going away is the coming home. But now, as I lie on the sand with someone nervously holding me still, all I can think is, 'Will I ever again be able to do the things I love doing with my family – the riding, the skiing, setting up the cricket stumps in one of the paddocks or blasting a ball into the back of the net in the back garden?'

Trying youngsters is all part and parcel of my job, so jumping on-board the well-bred five-year-old was no different. Funny, though, she wasn't the horse I'd been recommended to go and see at this yard. I'd spotted her in the stable, asked the owner about her and liked the sound of her sufficiently for me to try her. I still don't know exactly what happened when I fell off – and people seem reluctant to tell me. "You really don't want to know, Tim," they say – so I guess it was bad. But more about that later. What I do remember is a sickening feeling as I was carted towards the short end of the arena. 'This isn't going to end well,' I thought. I recall the unnerving feeling of sliding sideways and falling backwards at the same time, and feeling helpless in the knowledge that I couldn't do anything about it – I was going to hit the deck. Then the next thing I was aware of was my head being cradled by someone.

Would I still be involved in the career that has given me the opportunity to represent my country on numerous occasions on Nations Cup teams, at the World Equestrian Games, European Championships and, of course, the Beijing Olympics in 2008? It's a huge honour for me to represent my country and before the accident happened – just nine months before the London 2012 Games – there was already a buzz of excitement and optimism on the Northamptonshire yard of Team Stockdale. Preparations were already under way for the historic event.

The 2012 Olympic team was, without a shadow of a doubt, the team I wanted to be on for obvious reasons. There was certainly never going to be another Olympics in the UK in my lifetime – and maybe not even in the kids' lifetimes. In a way, it seemed as though my life had always been building to the London Olympics – it had the potential to be the highlight of my career. But waiting for the ambulance to arrive, I wondered if it was all over, if it had all been for nothing. Would I even walk again?

"Keep his head absolutely still," instructs one of the paramedics. I guess at this point that I'm in a fairly bad way. I'm at the side of the arena, covered in a blanket and drifting in and out of consciousness. I don't know where I am and have no idea who any of the people are around me. Funnily enough, I'm not in a huge amount of pain – that's not the main issue. But I complain of relentless, unforgiving pins and needles down the right-hand side of my body – from my right shoulder, down my right arm and all the way down my side to my leg. They are so bad that I ask if I can change my position, naively thinking that I am lying awkwardly and stopping the blood flow. Of course, though, I know now that it was my bruised spinal cord warning me as to the extent of the damage.

The paramedic wouldn't let me move and I remember thinking what a prat he was for being unreasonable and not allowing me to get comfortable. But the worst was yet to come. Even to this day, just the memory of the ambulance crew strapping me to a body board makes my hands go clammy and my chest tightens with panic. Why? Because I'm claustrophobic and being strapped to a body board, unable to move a single muscle, is my idea of purgatory, as irrational a fear as it may seem. I was strapped in really tightly, obviously because they didn't want me moving and subsequently damaging my spinal cord further, which was perfectly reasonable. But my unreasonable fear of restraint and the realisation that my oxygen mask was taped to my face with plasters was enough to send me over the edge – paralysis or no paralysis. And when this irrationality kicked in, boy did it kick in.

I was okay for about the first hour-and-a-half and then came the complete paddy when I started thrashing about. I had a panic attack and was telling them – not asking, but demanding – that they had to get the mask off me. So one of the crew unfastened a strap so that I could move one of my arms, just a little bit, but it was enough to quell the panic and allow me to regain control of my fear. Thankfully – probably more so for the ambulance crew than myself – I was able to keep my claustrophobia in check, although I was dripping with sweat by this stage. However, the thought of the journey nearly being over kept me just about sane – at least until the driver started to accelerate.

"I'm glad we're on the main road now, we can get some speed up," he said.

I couldn't believe it – we'd only just made it off the mountain after all that time. It had taken the ambulance the best part of an hour to do the mile-and-a-half descent from the yard, crawling down at a snail's pace, the driver gingerly snaking his way over the rough, mountainous terrain, trying to avoid every bump and pothole, so as not to jolt my battered body unnecessarily. I despaired, but tried desperately to reason with myself. These guys were experts, they knew what they were doing, they realised that the slightest bump could compound my injury even further and land me in a wheelchair for life. No amount of my complaining or fussing about claustrophobia was going to help. I had to shut up and get on with it. And we'd still got another hour-and-a-quarter to go before we reached our destination – Shrewsbury Hospital.

I just remember thinking, 'I don't know if I can do this, I can't bear this'. Then with no other options left to me, I tried to muster a smile. In my world, there's no such word as 'can't'. If I had a pound for every time I've said that... anyway. Here I was, descending into a negative spiral, gloom and depression setting in as the restraining straps started to bite into me and the severity of my condition became real in my mind. This was one long, hard journey. It was arduous and never-ending as I lay there suppressing my panic and imagining the worst. I knew I'd broken my neck and told the paramedic as much.

"Don't be silly, you don't know that," he said.

"I do, I know I have. I've broken my bloody neck."

Arriving at the hospital couldn't have come quickly enough, even if it was only to confirm what I already suspected.

"I've broken enough bones in my body to know what I've done," I told the doctor who examined me initially. "I've broken my neck," I told him assuredly.

As if to confirm my self-diagnosis, when he felt around the back of my head, I knew immediately that I was correct, because the pain was unbearable and unforgiving. The plan was obviously to X-ray my neck, not so much to confirm what I'd done but to see how bad the break was. While I waited to be wheeled into X-ray, I had time to think. I was convinced I'd broken my neck so had to keep still, I wasn't to panic because I needed to keep a clear head and think about who needed to be contacted: Dr Peter Whitehead, Team Doctor for the British Equestrian Olympic and Paralympic Teams; Will Connell, British Equestrian Federation Performance Director, and Team Leader for the Athens Olympics 2004 and Beijing 2008; and Rob Hoekstra, Chef d'Equipe of the British showjumping team.

In the meantime, however, Laura was on her way and all I could do was wait. I wanted her here, not just to see a familiar face to encourage me, tell me everything would be okay and to get some answers from the doctors, but because I felt alone, confused, frightened. My mind started to play tricks on me as I battled to recall the events of the day. I had no idea what time it was, and felt frustrated and angry with myself for not being able to piece it all together. I felt I was losing control as a gamut of emotions played havoc with my memory, as I suddenly became aware of the pain, the excruciating pain that was claiming my body.

As I lay on that trolley waiting to go into X-ray, alone, staring at the white ceiling, unable to move, the fluorescent lighting hurt my eyes and served as a stark reminder as to why I was there. The harsh light made me blink and my eyes water. I realised they were tears, tears of frustration, tears for fears of the unknown, the future – if I still had one as a showjumper. I'd always envisaged my career ending in a blaze of glory, maybe after a major competition and an official announcement: 'Tim Stockdale has decided to retire from international showjumping.' I like to plan things and be in control of my destiny, so I'd always maintained that when it came down to the last chapter, there'd be a correct way of writing it and wrapping things up.

My mind was buzzing and it hurt because I couldn't separate one thought from another. It was as if my life was flashing before my eyes, before the final curtain came down. All the good times, the great times, the triumphs were whirling around – and strangely enough the memory of my first-ever rosette when I was 11, not of falling off a five-year-old horse. I remember telling everyone at school about my rosette and rather than call me a sissy for riding horses, they were proud, intrigued and interested.

All these thoughts and memories flooding my mind… how much I wanted to experience them all again… I wasn't ready for it to end. Any retirement plans were going to be on my terms – I want to ride off into the sunset with a big, fat cigar and a glass of my favourite Rioja. Not because I'd fallen off a five-year-old horse and bust my neck. No, my retirement was going to be on my terms, this is not supposed to be the last chapter, it's not supposed to end like this…

Chapter 2

I hated riding because it hurt!

- My tough upbringing
- School didn't do it for me
- Looking for trouble
- Out to work, aged nine

If, as a youngster, anyone had suggested that I'd end up riding horses for a living – and go to an Olympic Games – I'd have told them they needed their head testing. I would also have said that there was more chance of me flying to the moon than there ever was of me sitting on a horse, let alone jumping one over some crazy, huge fences to earn a few pounds. Besides, I didn't like riding because it hurt and I hated horses even more because they smelled funny and had minds of their own. Why on earth would I want to waste my time on these oafish creatures when I could be out playing cricket or football instead? And to think that some people rode them for pleasure... unbelievable!

I'd come from a family of builders, so the chance of me following Dad into his profession was more than likely. No, the only reason why my twin brother Ivan and sister Marie and I ever got involved with these creatures was when Mum packed us off to the local riding school during the summer holidays. We were getting under her feet and she'd had enough of us all moping around the house. We were usually pretty good at amusing ourselves, but tempers had been running high that day and poor

Mum had had enough of us all picking on one another.

One of identical twin boys, I was born on 12 August, 1964, in Kilton Hospital, Worksop, South Yorkshire, a full 25 minutes ahead of my brother Ivan – a fact of which I was incredibly proud, according to Mum.

"But do you know why I'm older?" I'd ask anyone who'd listen.

Each time my mother would hold her breath, wondering what would come out my mouth this time.

"Because I came out of the ambulance first," I'd say proudly.

Even at that tender age, I was outspoken and knew my own mind and was never afraid to let people know what I thought. Things never change.

We had three older brothers, Stuart, Kevin and Iain and later, a younger sister, Marie. From as far back as I can remember, we six kids enjoyed a relatively happy childhood in Retford, Nottinghamshire, where we lived with Mum (Nancy) and Dad (Geoff). But it was always me who'd be picked on and teased remorselessly by the older boys, probably because I was the gobby one and not afraid to stand my ground.

As a family, we were all keen swimmers and spent a lot of our spare time at the local swimming baths, where my two eldest brothers taught me to swim. Well, they'd chuck Ivan and me in to see which one of us would float the longest before we sank like weighted sacks to the bottom of the pool, spluttering and thrashing as we headed down into the murky depths. It was terrifying, but generally it was me who would stay afloat long enough to make my first feeble attempt at any recognisable stroke. But then that was what life was like in our household – sink or swim.

Coming from a family of eight, there was no shortage of laughter and no lack of back-chat, banter and jokes – but if I had a pound for every prank my elder brothers played on me, I'd be retired to a desert island by now. But because Ivan and I looked the same, we'd make the most of every opportunity to trick people into thinking I was him and he was me. Although that was probably about as mischievous as it got for us, blaming one another for things we'd done and enjoying people's confusion as they tried to tell us apart.

However, when my three elder brothers weren't picking on Ivan and me, they were leading us astray. They had, for instance, fathomed out how to get into the swimming baths without paying and considering that we were there every single day, that saved our parents a heap of money – although we did it because we could more than anything else. So Ivan and I were swiftly moulded into miniature versions of Stuart and Kevin as they showed us the ropes, deftly prying open the back door at the pool and jamming a foot in so that we could all pile in before the door shut automatically.

Stuart was a tough lad and would think nothing of fighting friends or family for something he wanted. At times we'd all fight and argue as if our lives depended on it and while it probably sounds worse than it was, Ivan and I soon realised that being backward in coming forward meant that you'd lose out. The competition was fierce and relentless, but it toughened me up.

Learning to stand up for myself was good preparation for school, which was something I looked forward to. I wanted to make new friends and spend time with kids my own age. Although infant school – Grove Street Infants – was pretty uneventful, even at the tender age of five we learnt to fend for ourselves, walking the $2\frac{1}{2}$ miles to school through busy Retford, accompanied by Kevin and Iain who were only young teenagers themselves. No one gave it a second thought, it was the norm – until perhaps the day Ivan fell in the canal, leaving Mum more furious about the state of his school uniform than anything else.

We lived in the middle of Retford until I was seven. Dad was in the building trade – a bricklayer – and his father had been a carpenter, so that probably explains why, if I hadn't been a showjumper, I'd have chosen the same profession. It was in the blood and also the reason why I still love DIY.

When I've got some spare time in-between shows and teaching, I love to go around the yard and paddocks at home repairing and painting fences, banging nails in here, there and everywhere. And whenever I come across a tool tradestand at a county show, wild horses can't drag me away until I've been tempted by some new-fangled gadget or power tool to add to my ever-growing collection at home.

Dad was a truly skilled builder and the Stockdales – every male member of my family except me and Ivan, who both followed a different career path – have an exemplary reputation in the area for professionalism and good workmanship. In fact, it was Dad who built our house at 175 Albert Road. He'd demolished the original house and rebuilt another on the same plot. Then when we later moved to the country – again with his usual flair and good eye for properties with potential – he bought two little, run-down, semi-detached cottages in Pinfold Lane, Welham – just outside Retford – and knocked them into one.

While our departure to the country was to kick-start a number of new interests for me, it also meant a move away from our best friend, Felice Gallucci. Although we weren't at the same infants school, our houses were about 50 yards apart and our mums became friends when they met on the maternity ward in Kilton Hospital, bringing the three of us into the world. So there started a great friendship between the two families, not least between me, Ivan and Felice. The three of us would hang out together after school doing what little boys did best – getting dirty, looking for mischief and ending up in all sorts of scrapes. But we were invincible and called ourselves The Retford Reds, imagining ourselves carrying out all sorts of secret missions!

As the terrible threesome, we used to go down to the local coal drops where they unloaded coal from the trains and ride our bikes up and down the black, sooty mountains. We would get filthy in the swirling dust clouds, returning home as black as your hat. We'd ride under the railway bridges, even alongside the tracks – health and safety wasn't big in those days – then raft across the local river, the Trent, on a makeshift raft looking for adventure.

From Grove Street Infants, we were sent to Carr Hill Junior from the age of seven to eleven. I didn't buy into the idea of school and wasn't particularly gifted academically, but then I wasn't a complete dunce. And while I wasn't the most rebellious pupil, I wouldn't do things just for the sake of it. I was more a leader than a follower and was always questioning, which I'm sure drove the teachers mad. But my relentless questions were because I wanted to expand my knowledge and understanding by refusing to take anything at face value. I'm still like that today.

On the whole, though, I enjoyed my time at Carr Hill Junior and am especially grateful to them for igniting my passion for sport and football in particular. When I wasn't having run-ins with teachers and running amok with Ivan and Felice, I could be found honing my football skills. I was a voracious supporter of the game and couldn't get enough of it, but then that's not surprising, because we were a footballing family and the interest obviously rubbed off. I recall being a ferocious tackler, something that poor Ivan would testify to, when I was so determined to wrestle the ball from him that I careered straight into him and ended up breaking his leg. I'd managed to run him down from a good 50 yards and was going so fast that I couldn't have stopped even if I'd wanted to. It was horrific.

As a family, we were very good at sport and my commitment to football paid off when I was picked for the Carr Hill Junior School football team at the age of nine. I remember feeling so proud as I walked out onto the pitch to take my place in goal. I wasn't particularly big, but I was quick and cat-like and had no fear in throwing myself to the ground to keep the ball out of the net. During my first game against a rival local team, the whole school stopped their lessons to come out and cheer us on. It was quite a big crowd for a nine-year-old to play in front of, but I loved it – even though we lost 5-2.

Cricket also played a big part in our lives, Dad being an ardent supporter of the game and competent player. It's something I still have a fanatical interest in today, although more as a spectator than a participant. In fact, such was my cricketing prowess at Carr Hill that I became team captain at the age of 11. But it was a day of mixed emotions for me – I was euphoric at leading the team out onto the pitch but gutted when we lost. So while I was never an academic star at school, I excelled on the sports field.

With the move to the country came a lot of new ventures – not least the horses – which up until this point hadn't featured in my life at all. In fact, as a family we'd had nothing to do with animals or livestock, not even cats or dogs – certainly not since me and Ivan were babies anyway, when Mum and Dad had a St Bernard who once lay on top of Ivan and nearly squashed him. The nearest I'd ever come to anything remotely horsey was a donkey ride with Ivan on the beach at Weston-super-Mare one summer. Learning to ride wasn't so much a conscious decision for us, more something that was instigated by Mum to get Ivan and me out of her hair.

We'd been arguing about who had broken whose bike, but Mum's patience was wearing thin, so she ordered us either up to our room or off to the local riding school for a couple of hours to make ourselves useful. Neither option sounded in the least appealing, so with us moaning about life not being fair, she grabbed us by the scruff of our necks, chucked us in the back of the car, drove us down the road and dumped us on one bemused Anna-Lou Daybell, who ran Cherry Holt Riding School. Now Anna-Lou was a real stickler for detail and she ran a very good riding school – her standards were impeccably high and she'd settle for nothing short of perfection in all things. The establishment was really well-equipped and lessons were well-structured. There was a nice line of stables, some paddocks, a small arena and a handful of various hairy-looking ponies. Everything was clean and tidy and ran like clockwork.

But there was one problem – I didn't want to ride. I hated the idea, as did Ivan. The ponies were big, they smelled funny and you just never knew what they were plotting in their silly heads. I also hated riding because it hurt – every pinching, leg-bruising minute of it. But I didn't have the courage to say so out loud. So as far as the riding lessons were concerned, we had to grin and bear it – we were stuck with it, like it or lump it.

However, I discovered that there were more appealing opportunities for those of us who didn't want to ride. I came to the conclusion that the energy I wasted whingeing about riding could be channelled into something I did enjoy doing, like odd jobs for Anna-Lou, helping her tidy up the yard, repair fences and paint the showjumps – jobs that required a steady hand and a sharp eye. I was in my element, until all my offers to help Anna-Lou keep the yard shipshape backfired on me. In return for all my labour, I was given free riding lessons, the last thing I wanted. Why couldn't they understand that I just wanted to help out and run around the place? I didn't give a monkey's about the riding – until, that is, one evening when I helped turn the ponies out.

It was a ritual at the end of the day, when two or three of us would each take a pony, throw a headcollar on and ride bareback to the field along a 600-yard private track – the perfect racetrack. I was told by one of the older girls that we could have a gentle canter along the track. So as soon as we hit grass, I kicked my pony into canter and he was off, galloping along the track as fast as his little legs could carry him. I was riding one pony and leading another that day, and taken completely by surprise – it was sheer hell and I was terrified.

But then a peculiar thing happened. This feeling of fear gave way to excitement, then pleasure and fun as we hurtled along the track. I was actually starting to enjoy it, the speed, the exhilaration, the control, the confidence of being able to stay on. And more so once I'd charged all the way to the end of the track and told my ponies to 'whoa' and they obeyed. I'd never experienced that kind of power before. More often than not, I found it near-impossible to pick up a canter in a lesson in the school and it would only usually happen when my pony followed his pal, when I'd invariably end up running into the back of the ride.

But that day, I knew I'd made my pony canter by myself and I'd made him stop. This was a huge turning point for me. I was empowered. I was in control, rather than the pony taking charge. It was the best feeling in the world and I couldn't wait to get up to the riding school again and have another ride.

In no time at all, inspired by that experience, I really began to enjoy my riding – so much so that I decided to look for a job, my first paid job, at the age of nine. I wanted to learn more about these mysterious beasts first-hand. I knew that Mr Smith, the local scrap man who lived at the end of our lane, kept a few hunters, so I went along to ask his groom if I could have a Saturday job. So it was that I started work on Saturdays from

7am-2pm, and was paid the princely sum of 50p a week. Not a lot of money to be sure, but then that wasn't my objective. I wanted to be around the horses, and learn how to do things properly like clean tack, muck out and groom.

Mr Smith's groom, Tony Dobson, was very patient with me and showed me the ropes. He must have thought I had promise and a natural affinity with horses, or at least a real passion for it, because he took the trouble to tell Dad about a pony for me. His name was Danny Boy and apparently a perfect first pony. He was at Wellow Park Stables, owned by Margaret Willetts, and cost £50 including saddle and bridle. But Margaret would only sell him to us, the non-horsey family that we were, on the condition that we joined The Pony Club.

Chapter 3

Oh, Danny Boy...

● Pony in the potting shed
● My first showjumping experience
● Harvey Smith – in my fancy-dress class?
● My first and last Pony Club appearance

Danny Boy was 12.2hh, about 12 years old, brown and white. He came home the same day we saw him, only for Mum and Dad to realise that we didn't actually have a stable to put him in. So he ended up living in a garden shed that Dad had made, complete with potting shelf and a picturesque little window that looked out onto the garden. Although we'd obviously cleared out the shed before putting Danny in, it was a tight squeeze for the poor pony and only measured about 8ft by 4ft, with a raised step up into it. It was just about big enough for Danny Boy, as long as he didn't want to turn around. And whether or not he could lie down in it remains a mystery, as we never actually watched him.

So he lived in the shed and was as good as gold, not once objecting. We'd lead him in and could just about shut the door on his bottom, but every time we opened it, we were greeted by a pile of poo and, of course, he'd have to reverse out, carefully negotiating the step. Most ponies would have tripped or stumbled, but not Danny Boy. He picked up each foot carefully and deliberately, reversing out with amazing agility considering that he couldn't see where he was going. After much discussion, though, we decided to back him in. Then at least, Mum said, he'd have the pleasure of looking out over the door that had been specially adapted for him. So we set about teaching him how to reverse in, then in the mornings, it was easier to lead him out and of course he didn't have to trample his way through the pile of poo that was now at the back of the shed. Genius!

Right from the word go, Dad had drummed it into Ivan and me that Danny Boy was our responsibility. Dad had done his bit buying him, now it was up to us to do the rest. We were to look after him, feed him and ride him every single day, come rain or shine, because it wasn't fair for him to be kept in the shed all day long. We'd no land for turnout, just a back garden large enough to bowl a cricket ball in comfortably and a steep manmade hill at the back that we'd ride Danny Boy up and down, imagining it was the Hickstead Derby Bank.

When he first arrived on the scene, he'd been a bit naughty when it came to hacking, refusing point-blank to go down the drive. In fact, 'nappy' soon became his middle name. I remember Ivan trying his damnedest to get Danny Boy out of the drive, but the cheeky so-and-so would only show his disgust and obstinacy by rearing up, spinning around and high-tailing it back home. Try as he might, Ivan just couldn't get him on his side that day and it didn't help that the rest of the family had come out to spectate, lend support and voice their opinions on what was to be done – rich coming from an entirely non-horsey family. So I decided to have a go at getting Danny down the drive just as Grand-dad ambled up on his way back from his daily visit to the pub. As he moved steadily closer, I scrambled onto Danny Boy who planted himself in his usual manner, and no amount of kicking and shoving on my part could persuade him otherwise. Ears set stubbornly to the side, he just plain ignored me. I gave him a swipe with my stick and he replied with a rear. Grand-dad gave a little chuckle as he went by.

"What's goin' on here then, Timmy?" he asked, eyeing first the pony and then me.

"He doesn't want to go, Grand-dad. Look…" I gave Danny

Boy another boot for good measure to prove the point. The pony swished his tail, but other than that ignored me. Then with one swift movement, Grand-dad poked Danny Boy right up the bum with the pointy end of his umbrella. Not surprisingly, this sent him bolting, hell for leather, down the drive – and who wouldn't with an umbrella up their backside?

"There you go," exclaimed Grand-dad proudly, "our Timmy's made him go." And go Danny Boy did, without a second thought, until I was nothing more than a speck on the horizon to the amusement of the assembled group. I remember being completely shell-shocked at the time, and it was a good hour later that Mr Kay, the local farmer, rang my parents.

"I've got your son sitting on my front lawn on a brown and white pony," he told them, "and it's munching its way through my azaleas. The boy seems to be crying his eyes out; could you please come and retrieve him?" Notice that no-one had bothered to follow me on my runaway pony; they went about their business and assumed I'd turn up sooner or later.

That wasn't the only time Danny Boy ran off with me – in fact, he did it more often than not, but it was all valuable experience. He once took off with me at a local hunt and careered towards a ditch that was so overgrown with weeds that I didn't see it. Danny Boy did, however, deftly darting out to the right at the last minute, saving his own skin but not mine as I shot off head first into the ditch like an Olympic diver. He then galloped off with me in hot pursuit on foot. By the time he'd been caught and brought back to me as I trudged wearily after him, I'd been given a severe dressing-down from the Master of the hunt. I was told in no uncertain terms that I shouldn't go out hunting until I had control of my pony. The Master left me feeling so ashamed of our conduct that day, it left a mental scar with me for many, many years after.

While I realised it wasn't the done thing to be out of control and overtaking most of the members of the hunt staff, it's not as though I'd done it on purpose, or was doing it for a dare or a laugh. I'd been traumatised by the whole thing, truly terrified and I didn't like the feeling of being galloped off with one bit.

I needed reassurance, not angry words. I personally think the Master was out of order for giving an enthusiastic 10-year-old the telling off he did. It put me off big time and I ended up being frightened of going hunting. In fact, it wasn't until I was 17 or 18 that I felt ready to try again, and this time thoroughly enjoyed it.

When I think about it now, as a family we really hadn't got a clue what we were doing when it came to horses. Mum and Dad weren't horsey, but they'd thought nothing of going out to buy Danny Boy. I don't even think I rode him before we bought him. We just handed over the money. So I suppose it was entirely reasonable for the owner, Margaret Willetts, to sell us the pony with the proviso that we joined The Pony Club to learn about stable management, to watch for common ailments and be taught how to feed and muck out.

Joining The Pony Club – the Grove – was the start of great things, although it was also a complete revelation to us, opening up a whole, new, knowledgeable world. I remember our excitement at going to see the District Commissioner for the blue forms to fill in that would gain us entry to this exclusive club. She was known as 'Aunty Curtis', presumably because her name was Mrs Curtis, and she lived in a pretty cottage in Grove. She was a little, wizened old lady of about 80 and I remember being overjoyed when Mum bought us The Pony Club Manual, the tie and the badge, which I thought was the real stamp of approval and something I wore with pride.

My Pony Club 'Manual of Horsemanship' was like a bible to me and I'd read it from cover to cover, eventually realising that actually, a garden shed probably wasn't the best place to keep a pony. Even Dad agreed that Danny Boy, who'd been living in the shed now for about a month, shouldn't have to make do with his 'cosy' living quarters much longer, so he built us three lovely stables. And so it was that I embarked on this long journey of learning, making sure we did everything by the book.

While Danny Boy may have been a little git from time to time, we did have some fun together and probably provided a lot of laughs – and disbelief – to the horsey know-it-alls in our local community, I'm sure we were the source of great amusement. One such 'episode' involving me and Danny Boy occurred when Mum was driving back from shopping one summer's day along the busy main road to Gainsborough. There was a huge tail-back of traffic and everything was crawling along at a snail's pace – probably caused by a tractor, she thought. But no, when she finally reached the source of the hold-up, she found it was me and Danny Boy, returning from a day at the canal, trundling along at our own pace, shirtless and shoeless – I must have looked like a proper urchin. It was a long, hot summer that year and we were in the middle of a drought, so what was more sensible than riding down to the canal to cool off. I'd ride bareback along the main road, me in just my swimming trunks and riding hat, and Danny Boy in a headcollar. And I'd have a bucket slung over my shoulder so that he'd be able to have a drink when we got there.

We used to hack everywhere because we didn't have a trailer for Danny Boy. One year, we hacked to the Barnby Moor Show just outside Retford, all 7½ miles along main roads and Danny Boy with no shoes on, as we never shod him. It was one of the biggest events of the year, but turned out to be a wasted journey, because I got eliminated at the first fence in the minimus, my first-ever showjumping experience. I'm not surprised really, because Danny Boy wasn't a jumping pony, I didn't have a clue what I was doing and I'd had very little practice actually jumping jumps. But that seemed to be the pattern as far as competitions were concerned – I'd enter them, but can't remember ever jumping more than two fences in a row. What on earth possessed me to enter them, I'll never know.

We were totally clueless, making it all up as we went along. I'd had no jumping lessons as such and any practice we could get in-between competitions took place in our back garden, over old oil barrels. We had six of them and they were red with white stripes around the middle to give me something to aim for. We'd build a course of four jumps – two barrels on their side, followed by a barrel with a cross-pole, two more barrels on their side and then an upright with a barrel – and that was it. But depending on Danny Boy's mood on a given day, we mostly went around or through the jumps.

I may not have had much success jumping at Barnby Moor that day, but I did well in the fancy dress class, much to my amazement and that of my friends at Carr Hill Junior, who I impressed with a third-place rosette – my first-ever ribbon – that I'd won for turning up as a football hooligan. The weekend before, there'd been a fight between Manchester United and Leeds football fans. So I dressed up as a footballer and kitted Danny Boy out as a fan with a scarf around his neck, and plasters and fake blood all over us. Talk about gruesome. But we came third and I proudly took the rosette in to school to show my mates.

It was strange, though. None of my schoolfriends had ponies, yet surprisingly I came in for none of the teasing nor ridicule that you might expect about riding being a girl's sport. Instead, my classmates were in awe of me and more interested to know whether or not I knew Harvey Smith and if he'd been in the fancy dress class that day.

With me and Ivan starting to get out and about more to shows, however, it presented one problem – one pony, two riders. So Mum and Dad decided to get another one for us, which is when we heard about Titmus, a little grey 13hh pony that came to us on loan. He was fast, a right little galloper, but like Danny Boy, not much of a jumper. It was with Titmus, however, that I was asked – at about the age of 11 – to represent the Pony Club in the Prince Philip Cup Mounted Games near Lincoln. A couple of people had dropped out and I'd been earmarked for the job, possibly because I'd been to a lot of rallies and the organisers were getting to know me. But this was a big occasion for me and I felt out of my depth, as I didn't know any of my other team mates. And come the day of the show, rather than it being the triumph I'd envisaged, it turned out to be a day of embarrassing shame.

For weeks I had fretted and fussed about the upcoming show. I cleaned Titmus to within an inch of his life and polished my tack until it sparkled. Mum starched my white shirt and I tried to prepare myself mentally for the big day. As the show was in Lincoln, one of the other team members came to pick us up, but it was all this added kerfuffle of the occasion that only added to my tension as my Prince Philip Cup debut crept closer and closer.

My family came along to support me as usual so I really wanted to do well. Eventually, when it was time for our class, I was a bundle of nerves. The first event was the flag race and I was due to go third. I waited on the start line in anticipation of me and Titmus making a fast, flying start, then as our second team member galloped towards the line and whizzed passed me, I grabbed the flag, relieved that I hadn't made a fool of myself by dropping it. 'Phew, worst bit over,' I remember thinking as I sat tight and kicked Titmus on. But nothing happened. So I kicked again. Still nothing happened; he wouldn't go over the start line. The little so-and-so dug his heels in and napped as only he knew how to.

I was determined to get him going, so I turned the flag upside down and used it to give him a smack. Needless to say, this catapulted Titmus into action and we raced to the end, then turned around and galloped back to the finishing line, only to discover that rider number three – me – had been eliminated for smacking his pony with the flag. And that led to the whole team being eliminated. I was so heartbroken, not just to be eliminated but because no one had acknowledged what I thought was great ingenuity in the face of adversity. It made perfect sense to me. My pony wouldn't go, so I used the flag to encourage him. I thought it showed great initiative. But unsurprisingly, The Pony Club didn't see it that way and it turned out to be my one and only appearance for them – and I was a member until I was 15.

As I became more and more involved with The Pony Club scene, Ivan became less so although my sister, Marie, began to take up an interest. She joined and together we used to go off to rallies – and we loved them. And much as my parents still didn't know one end of a horse from another, they were unbelievably supportive. They'd come to all the shows and Pony Club rallies, and make a day of it, watching our classes, coming prepared with enough sandwiches to feed an army.

Certainly for the first year or so until we got our own transport, we'd have to hack to events. Then we'd be driven around in the trailer that Dad eventually bought. And what a luxury that was – gone were the days of a two-hour hack to an event, there and back. But at the time, that was all part 'n' parcel of owning a pony, and getting out there. All things considered, it was a miracle that we weren't injured or killed on the roads. Equally, it was a miracle that our ponies survived their time with us, given the limited extent of our knowledge. In fact, even to this day Dad still doesn't know the difference between hay and straw. And he still calls spurs stirrups and stirrups spurs.

"Are you going to put your stirrups on?" he once asked me, as I was about to jump the round of my life in the Longines King George V Gold Cup in 2010…

Chapter 4

The General Election changed my life

- Failing the Eleven Plus was perfect
- We were dunces
- Our impulse buy
- Eggs stopped my pony rearing

I have never been one to take anything for granted, even as a child. I realised that Ivan and I were extremely lucky to have all the things we had – the ponies, the trailer, parents who'd come to support us at events here, there and everywhere. But by this stage, there were clear divides appearing within the family. One half was interested in country pursuits and showjumping, the other in a passion for football, going out with mates and generally doing one's own thing. Stuart had married and moved away by this time. Kevin and Iain were still at home but working full-time and not into the ponies at all. But for me – and now Marie – they were a pivotal part of our daily life.

While Dad earned decent enough money with his own building firm, MBS, my parents made sure that we all understood the value of every penny. The houses we lived in were ones that Dad had built or renovated himself and if anything got broken, it was never replaced with new, but repaired. In fact, we made do and would mend a lot of stuff around the house. Our bikes were all hand-me-downs, and then he built the stables. These, by the way, weren't rickety buildings he'd bodged together – they were fine, sturdy buildings carefully planned and constructed. At Christmas, presents were often handmade. It was just the way it was. My sister, for example, was given a doll's house that Dad had hand-crafted himself and it was exquisite, a work of art with a tiled roof and a back section that came off. He had spent months painstakingly building it for Marie and the detail was incredible.

We may have had two okay cars, more than one telephone and a colour TV while none of our close friends did, but we rarely went abroad for our holidays and we didn't eat out in restaurants. Holidays were normally in the family caravan to somewhere like Tenby or the Lake District because Mum hated flying. A holiday treat involved going to the pub for a Coke and a packet of crisps. But even with holidays, we were very much a divided family, with me, Ivan and Marie going with Mum and Dad, while the elder brothers stayed at home. In fact, I can't actually remember going on holiday with Iain and Kevin ever. It was almost as if we were two families – us and them. I'm not sure if that was intentional, but it's something that hasn't changed to this day. The elder siblings hang out together, as do the younger ones. I guess the age gap had a lot to do with it –you just have more in common with those of a similar age to you.

Nothing changed, however, as far as the ponies were concerned, with us riding them every day and Dad helping with the mucking out. One thing that had changed by this stage, though, was school. I was now going to the local secondary school – Sir Frederick Milner's, affectionately known as Freddie's. I'd failed my Eleven Plus miserably and I remember Mum coming upstairs to our bedroom and throwing the door open wide. Ivan and I were still in bed.

"You've failed your Eleven Plus," she yelled. "You're dunces, just like the rest of this family." Passing your Eleven Plus meant a place at the local grammar school, but if you failed, Freddie's was the next best thing. As far as I was concerned, if it was good enough for Dad and my elder brothers, then it was good enough for me. The only member of the family who turned out to have any brains was Marie, but they had disbanded the Eleven Plus the year she was due to sit it. Mum, obviously dismayed that none of her offspring was going to grammar school, rang the Education Council and asked if her daughter could sit the now-defunct exam. For her own peace of mind, she wanted to know if one of her children would have passed it. But they refused and I imagine it was a huge blow to Mum at the time.

While I might not have been the most academic kid on the block, I was 'street smart' as they say – others might call it opportunistic, but I prefer entrepreneurial. Ironically, failing the Eleven Plus was probably going to be the smartest thing I'd ever done. Ending up at Freddie's was to be just one of many fortunate twists of fate that have shaped my life (and continue to do so), especially the time school closed for the day when I was 12...

In 1976, Freddie's was closed because it was being used as a polling station in the General Election that saw Jim Callaghan elected Prime Minister. Ivan, Marie and I were all off school for the day, charging around the house causing havoc and arguing over who was going to ride. Mum hadn't a clue what to do with us, so in the end, she bundled us into the car and took us down to the local cattle market for the day. We enjoyed going there to see the animals for sale – all sorts of cattle, all types of pony being shown off by the dealers for prospective buyers, of which Mum turned out to be one.

Buying Corky for us that day was certainly not the intention and it was undoubtedly an expensive way of entertaining three restless kids, but we weren't going to stop her. Mum told us that Grand-dad had bought him for us, although Dad always disputes this saying that he didn't have the money. Whatever the truth, £345 changed hands and Corky, a 13.2hh dun gelding was ours. But because we hadn't banked on getting a new pony that day, Corky being a bit of an impulse buy, we hadn't figured out how to get him home. So Mum drove back to get Danny Boy's saddle and bridle so that we could ride him back the five or so miles home from Retford to Welham. But the bridle didn't fit Corky's massive head, so we ended up having to buy a new one anyway.

Not surprisingly, because Corky wasn't shod, he was really foot-sore by the time we reached home. He could barely put one foot in front of the other, so the local vet came out to examine him. After telling us that our lovely new pony was lame, which even to us novices was pretty obvious, he checked him over more thoroughly and told us that the pony we'd just bought was only three years old and had probably only just been backed – if at all. Such was our ignorance, however, that the significance of this discovery didn't register – it had just been a case of get on and get home. At the time, though, it spoke volumes for Corky's disposition and we thought that we'd got ourselves a nice, uncomplicated pony. But that was soon to change as Corky found his feet.

Although I devoted lots of time to Corky, he became a bit naughty with me after we got to know each other a little better, but it was down to me alone to work out a training plan for him and master all his quirky little ways – the nappiness, the rearing, the galloping off. I shall have to re-break him, I thought, so I taught him everything I'd learnt from my Pony Club manual. It was hard work, but Marie was riding Danny Boy more then, so that helped take the pressure off me having to exercise two ponies after school.

One of the vices I tried to cure Corky of was his rearing – he was like a circus pony on two legs. In fact, he was probably on two legs more than he was on four. I remember him rearing for all he was worth when we were out on one of my favourite hacks – The Baulk – which was the long, straight Roman road at the back of our house. At the end of it was a crossroads – go right for the short track home, left for the longer ride back through some of the villages. Of course, Corky wanted to go right, while I wanted to track left so I tried to persuade him that left was the better option. But he was having none of it and he tried to scare me by standing up. I wasn't easily frightened, though – in fact, it became a bit tedious for me, a real chore.

I really tried to break him of this habit, as it was beginning to get a bit silly by this stage – I'd end up spending half the hack stationary or with Corky on his back legs, so I decided to try the age-old trick of cracking a few raw eggs over his head. Although I don't remember where I'd heard about this cure, I knew for sure that I hadn't read about it in my Pony Club manual – I dare say I'd have been ex-communicated if the District Commissioner had heard about it. Anyway, I nicked some eggs from the larder and kept a stash in my pocket. The idea is that when you break the egg between their ears, the pony feels the egg running down his face and thinks he's hit his head and that he's bleeding, so he stops rearing. I'm not sure I'd advocate the same technique today, but it certainly did the trick then.

But for all those 'brick wall' moments, we had some great times together and would go off on day-long picnic hacks, with my rucksack on, packed full of food and drink. I'd also put my stirrups up and go for a gallop along The Baulk – it was about a mile-and-a-half long, with grass verges and a little trench every 10 or 15 metres that we'd jump. Then we'd get to the end and gallop back, sparks flying off the road as Corky would anticipate the start as we repeated the exercise. It was great fun racing along those grass verges, imagining I was a jockey running at Aintree. I can't say it was much fun for poor Corky, though, because he hadn't been clipped and would end up covered in sweat, puffing and blowing like a steam train! But I found it difficult to wipe the big, stupid grin off my face.

I also taught him how to jump, building a cross-country course in the woods out of wooden pallets and as many old branches as I could lay my hands on, a stepping stone for a few low-key one-day events – me dressed in a blue jumper with a blue knitted cover over my battered old hat. The seasoned competitors had their crash helmets and fancy silks, but I must have looked a right sight in something that resembled an oversized tea cosy. However, I thought I was the bee's knees in my home-made 'silk' and ubiquitous Stylo rubber riding boots – they were superb, I was certain I looked the part and had hit the big time.

Across country, Corky would always go clear, but we were far too slow and it was the dressage phase that always let us down. I just didn't buy into the dressage. It was complete nonsense in my book as we'd just go round in circles with Corky star-gazing. In fact, I can honestly say that I never once got him on the bit, or even really understood the concept then, and the only time he ever got close to getting his head down was to eat grass.

But showjumping was a different thing altogether. He may have been a common little pony, but there was nothing Corky wouldn't jump and nothing he wouldn't at least have a go at. In fact, at the first-ever Pony Club camp that Marie and I went to – at Osberton – Corky and I really came into our own as we took on all these enormous jumps. There was a Normandy bank, two really testing fences coming down a steep hill, a couple of solid-looking tree trunks and a massive double. I'd never seen anything like it, let alone tackled anything like it, but at the end of the day I was the only person in the Pony Club who'd jumped this formidable double. Corky was unfazed by anything and he loved his jumping. He was still only five years of age, but he was one of the bravest ponies I've ever come across. He was phenomenal.

Luckily for me, the Grove turned out to be a very good branch of The Pony Club and I continued to read my Pony Club manual from cover to cover. I never tired of it and loved reading about ponies, enthusiastically making up management charts and training programmes for my ponies, keeping tab of our successes and the failures, when and where things went wrong and why I thought they had in my very limited experience. In fact, this is something I've carried forward to my business today – I'm forever making lists, and like to plot and plan my horses' progress, and see at a glance how they're all doing. Of course, this organisation and planning was ingrained in me from a very early age by Dad, and it certainly helped that I am, by nature, a grafter.

My whole childhood was taken up with my ponies – they were never a chore, never something I got tired of doing. Very rarely did I complain about having to get up at 7am each day to ride them before school. I'd go out on the coldest and darkest of mornings with my balaclava on, looking like Darth Vader, but I didn't care what I looked like because I used to get bloody cold ears – they're big old things. Every time I went out there in the crisp morning air, I knew that riding Corky was going to be anything but straightforward and our ride was usually fraught with problems as he'd nap or run off with me. But never once did I think of giving up and even in those early days, at 12 years of age, horses were fast becoming a way of life for me. I can't ever remember missing a morning's ride and Dad would always make sure I took the ponies out for their morning constitutional.

"If you have an animal, you can't leave it inside – it's cruel," Dad would say and he was right.

Even now I still think it's cruel to keep a horse in its stable all day long. So when any of my horses are on box rest, I feel truly sorry for them. On my yard at home, the horses go out every single day – whether they're being exercised, hacked, led out for a bit of in-hand grazing or are out on the walker. I'm not one for leaving horses in the stable for two or three days without even thinking about it. It's just not natural.

With all this poring over books and self-taught horse husbandry, you'd think that I would have passed my Pony Club tests with flying colours. Not so. I'm ashamed to say that although I passed my D Test, I failed my C Test – one of the most basic certificates – not once, but twice. To be honest, it came as no surprise to me, because I was rubbish at anything involving exams. I expect, though, that if I'd put as much time and effort into school as I did into the ponies, I would have come out with a few more GCEs. Anyway, despite failing the C Test, I still became an international showjumper so I must have been doing something right and picked up a few skills along the way.

The Grove Pony Club also spawned some excellent talent in riders such as the late eventer Caroline Pratt, Jonny Beardsall who's now a journalist with 'The Telegraph' and international eventer Sarah Kellard. But I can pretty much guarantee that no one from that Pony Club would ever have thought they had an Olympian in their midst. If anyone had been challenged to pick out someone who, in 20 or 30 years' time would be at the Beijing Olympics or jumping in a world championship class, they would probably have picked one of the others. They would not, in a million years, have picked me… I guarantee it.

Nevertheless, I adored The Pony Club and it turned out to be one of the best experiences of my life. I used to enjoy camps and rallies, and was very competitive in all aspects of riding, if not life in general. Whether it was racing down a jumping lane, or taking off your saddle and bridle or mucking out in the fastest time possible, or carrying the most water buckets, I always had to win – and often did. Gradually my persistence paid off and with some regular outings to unaffiliated shows, I got a few wins under my belt – that really fuelled my passion for competition.

I competed at a lot of local shows – organised by, for example, Sherwood Hall Saddle Club, Saxonby Riding Club and Tick Hill Riding Club – and became a member of the Silver Horseshoe Riding Club. It may sound like a flowery name that no normal teenage boy would want to be associated with, but it was an excellent club with regular shows on Newark Showground, and was extremely well organised. They also provided some of the best trophies and rosettes around, which was the main reason I joined. We'd enter as many classes as we could in a day and collect as many ribbons as possible, to string up across the front of the car window so that everyone could see them.

By that stage, Marie was coming to the shows on her own pony. Dad had bought her a little chestnut called Sunshine – obviously Sunny for short – as Titmus and Danny Boy had been moved on. I'm ashamed to say that I can't remember what happened to either of them, but I imagine Danny Boy went off to another novice rider to be their first pony.

We were really lucky to have such generous parents. What has always amazed me is how devoted and selfless they were in supporting our riding interest, paying for everything that was required for what is, let's face it, an expensive and time-consuming hobby. But once they realised that this was beginning to turn into more of a way of life than a passing fad, everything I received at Christmas was for my ponies. I'd get a new rug, a new headcollar, a new grooming kit. We didn't get pocket money in those days because we had the ponies and all the trappings, but Grand-dad would give us what he called 'Saturday's money'. Of course, much as we were grateful for it, the amount he gave us wasn't exactly going to change our world. Up until the day he died when I was 16 – he was in his 90th year – he gave each of us kids 2p a week. He obviously thought it was a lot of money, but all it could buy was a couple of penny chews! Of course, it's the thought that counts, and I used to save mine up to buy Polos for Corky.

I suppose it would be easy to argue that I missed out on other childhood hobbies and toys because of the ponies, but I didn't care because they were the mainstay of my life and I was happy. I recall my utter joy at being given a brand new jute rug for Corky one Christmas – I remember sniffing it cautiously and breathing in its distinctive smell, and admiring the real leather strap at the front. And I recall Mum going to the sales at the Army & Navy Stores in Retford. She came home with a small, striped blanket for Corky that I thought was a Witney, but it wasn't – it was a really thin blanket, not the proper wool version. Yet, I remember thinking how fantastic it was to own a Witney.

For all my parents' lack of horsey experience, they were actually keen to learn from us – they trusted us from an early age to do the right thing for our ponies and that's quite a leap of faith. But it was those early days, the whole business of becoming a horse owner at a young age, that shaped the future and my life as it is now – which is why I think that 'doing it all ourselves' and learning as we went along was seminal for me and my story. Essentially it sowed the seed. And while I don't believe in fate, what happened that day when our school was used as a polling station for the General Election has been key in shaping my life's direction. That, and the evening I sneaked out of my bedroom as a 12-year-old and sat at the top of the stairs watching a television programme that was destined to change my life.

Chapter 5

Truly inspirational Chainbridge

- Emulating my heroes
- Building our horsebox
- Qualifying for Hickstead
- I stitched my own hand

I don't think showjumper Mike Saywell knows what a huge impact he has had on me and my life. Initially, it was seeing him winning a big class on TV that started it all and set wheels in motion. It was a school night and I should have been tucked up in bed and asleep, but the volume on the television was turned up loud enough to arouse my curiosity. I could just about make out the sharp intakes of breath as the audience gasped, then cheered and applauded. Their excitement was tantalising. My parents were watching The Royal International, which had become a family favourite and David Vine, of course, was hosting it. In those days, the show went out just after the nine o'clock news and I'd always plead with my parents to let me stay up for it. I'd been allowed to watch the first 10 minutes, after which I was officially dispatched to bed.

I'd laid there for a few minutes in the dark, listening to the hum of the TV coming from below, before I got up again. It was worth the risk, I decided, of incurring the wrath of my parents to catch a glimpse of Wembley Arena. I had to know what was going on. I crawled quietly out of bed and crept along the landing, terrified in case the floorboards creaked and gave the game away. The stairs were open-tread and if I cranked my head and neck just so, I could see through them to the TV. And what I saw next had a monumental impact on me.

Mike Saywell was riding Chainbridge in the 1976 King George V Gold Cup. My eyes fixed on the screen just at the moment he put in a daring turn back to a massive combination which he jumped clear to win the competition. It was mesmerising stuff and I had to stop myself from cheering and applauding with the rest of the Wembley crowd. Then David Vine interviewed Mike afterwards and they replayed the winning round to the famous music as the credits were rolling. The timing was perfect and he galloped through the finishing line as the music reached its climax − priceless.

I scuttled back to bed, full of awe and wonder, thinking about Mike and Chainbridge. How glorious they looked! I didn't know the guy from Adam, but I just lay there thinking to myself, 'That was fantastic. I want to do that one day. I would love to win that trophy and stand there in front of all those people.' Some riders talk about how the Hickstead Derby is their ultimate aim, but from that day forth, it was, for me, the King George V Gold Cup. Seeing Mike Saywell win in front of a partisan home crowd was the turning point. I had been truly inspired.

Realistically, though, I had about as much chance of doing that as I did of flying to the moon. If The Royal International was to become a serious proposition, I needed to be jumping top-level ponies and winning junior championships, but at that stage, this 12-year-old Pony Clubber hadn't jumped higher than a barrel! If anything was to inspire me that night when I watched Mike from the top stair, it was the fearless way he rode the course − an occasion that turned out to be a milestone in my young life and one I've never forgotten. I remember being captivated by the horse's strength and power − and the way the rider was in complete control and at one with his terrific jumping machine. It made such a lasting impression on me that every morning when I rode, I'd imagine myself at The Royal International with David Vine doing the commentary and introducing me to the millions of enthusiasts who were obviously watching me on TV.

"And Tim Stockdale has just cleared the combination to take the King George V Gold Cup" I could hear David saying in my head.

I'd canter Corky along the grass verge, humming the distinctive theme tune, imagining what it must be like to ride in front of a crowd cheering you on to victory.

I hadn't been a particular fan of Mike before I saw his round at Wembley, although I knew who he was – just as I did the other big names on the circuit. Indeed, most people knew the names of the top riders in showjumping back in those days as the sport was much more high profile. David Broome, for example, was one of my big heroes because of his finesse and I loved Harvey Smith because of his attitude and style. In fact, I used to carry my whip like Harvey, with it sticking out to the side. Then I'd try to emulate Eddie Macken's legs – he had great legs and still does! Eddie's lower leg never moved an inch and he sat so still on his horses. I'd even pat Corky the way Graham Fletcher used to reward his horses with a great slap on the neck for doing well. I didn't just aspire to be one rider in particular – I wanted to be all of them, stealing a little piece from each in order to be the ultimate rider.

In truth, I was just in awe of showjumping in general and a real groupie, knowing all the horses' names, and their likes and dislikes. But while I was a complete anorak, I didn't get many autographs because, as a family, we didn't go to many big shows. We did, however, win tickets for Olympia although I don't remember how. My brother, Kevin, took me down to London because Dad was busy. We watched football pundit Jimmy Hill riding in the pairs relay and he rode quite well. Then we watched the main class that featured all the big-name riders, many of whom were my heroes, but it was actually Kevin who'd had to point out to me that I'd only been standing next to German showjumping legend Alwin Schokemohle the whole time.

One outing that we loved going on as a family was to

Burghley for the three-day eventing and showjumping. We'd take the caravan and stay for a few days for a bit of a holiday. We'd do the usual things like walk the cross-country course and watch some of the dressage, but it was the showjumping that really caught our attention. The top names all went – Nick Skelton, Liz Edgar, Harvey Smith and Mike Saywell, all vying for the big-money prizes. And it didn't take my dad long to work out the maths.

Unlike the Burghley Horse Trials we know today, there used to be two days of showjumping with the chance to win anything from £300 to £600 in each of about half a dozen classes held during the show. First prize for the eventers, however, was around £1,500, which only one person could win. So with the showjumping, there was more than one chance of winning a decent prize and that alone was enough to convince my dad that showjumping was the way forward for me to eke out a living.

"You know, Son," said Dad, "you could earn a living out of this showjumping malarkey. Stick to that – forget the eventing."

Ironically, it had been eventing that I'd really wanted to pursue because having to master the three disciplines of dressage, cross-country and showjumping was a real test of good horsemanship – maybe a romantic idea for a 12-year-old, but perhaps not one you could rely on to bring home the bacon. It's still very much my belief today, eventing is more of a pastime, showjumping more of a profession. So after Dad's financial revelations, I realised that if I wanted to make anything like a serious living out of horses, I'd need to focus on showjumping. So we upped the ante, abandoning the mounted games and handy pony classes for opens and 'Chase Me Charlie', something that Corky was particularly good at as he could clear 4ft 6in with ease. But then as I started to win more trophies and as much as Corky was a cracking pony, fit for any enthusiastic Pony Clubber to have a lot of fun on, it soon became apparent that what I really needed was more of a jumper. This is where Maurice Fenton came in.

He was the local hay and straw merchant, but he did a bit of horse and pony dealing as well. Now Maurice owned a really good mare called Ferona who, at one time, had been ridden by John Whitaker. I went to have a ride on this big, black mare, the first time I'd ever ridden a horse. I remember Maurice being very complimentary about my riding, saying I had a natural gift and good hands. While I didn't ride Ferona again, however – she actually went off to Lionel Dunning – Maurice told my dad about a pony he thought we should consider. She was called Sweet Sue VIII and she'd originally been ridden by Michael Whitaker, after which she was sold to a young rider. The mare had started to stop and was quite quirky as I later discovered. Nonetheless, Dad and I went off with Maurice to try this pony, stupidly buying her for £400 on the strength of jumping her over just two jumps – it was ridiculous.

Sweet Sue was 14.2hh and a bay-roan mare, a bit of an ugly critter but in her heyday, she'd obviously been a very good jumping pony. I took her to all the little local shows and things started to go right for me, even though she wasn't the bravest pony in the world and would stop if she felt anxious about anything. But if you could muster a bit of confidence yourself and ride her accurately, then she'd go well.

Riding Sweet Sue well turned out to be a bit of a learning curve for me, because she was a tough cookie and very different to the ponies I'd had before. She had a few little quirks and foibles, so I learnt how to ride her in a specific way and soon got to know when and why the wheels would occasionally fall off. Of course, because Dad wasn't horsey, he relied on me to analyse these situations and work things out for myself. He couldn't tell me or teach me, because he didn't know, but that all came naturally to me because I've always been inquisitive. I've always questioned why things haven't worked out as they should have done. I've always analysed situations till I'm blue in the face and have never been one to accept things at face value.

What was becoming evident, however, was that we always seemed to find ourselves with problem ponies, ones who had issues and ones who other people hadn't been able to ride and retrain for whatever reason. Maurice, in his wisdom, obviously thought me and Sweet Sue might make a good partnership, because I seemed to have a knack with tricky, temperamental, nappy or unconfident ponies. Nevertheless, when we got it right, there wasn't a better feeling in the world.

One of my favourite show centres was Mill Lodge in Wisbech, Cambridgeshire, and I loved competing there with Sweet Sue. Some big local names were also there – like Paul Sutton, Annette Lewis, Keith Shore, Mark and Philip Heffer – and I loved the idea of rubbing shoulders with them, pretending I was one of the in-crowd, which of course I wasn't. We'd turn up in a scrappy, old blue lorry with a distinctive white dome on the top which Dad had converted from a railway wagon. Much as I loved our makeshift lorry, it was in stark contrast to the luxurious monster trucks with sponsors' names emblazoned on the side that stood proudly in the lorry park. We just couldn't compete with that lot.

Ever the builder and restorer, Dad had always reckoned on a railway wagon making a great horsebox. Originally, it had looked like a bit of a bus, with an area where the railway workers would sit upfront and a workstation at the rear. It had no power steering and may have been too low at the back to even accommodate a pony, but this was easily remedied with Dad's know-how as he simply made the roof higher, hence the distinctive white dome. Then he spruced up the blue bodywork with some white, 'go-faster' stripes painted on either side – a joke in itself really because on a good day, with the wind behind us and travelling downhill, we could only reach a maximum speed of 40mph. But I can't tell you how much I loved that lorry. It only had one seat and that was for the driver, so I used to sit in the front on a box that held all my brushes, and Mum would be in the back on a bench seat.

The travelling time didn't ever deter us, though, because Mill Lodge was such an electric place for me – and no more so than at Christmas and New Year. In fact, one year I was desperate to go to their New Year show because there were some qualifiers I wanted to have a go at. The entries weren't cheap, but my parents agreed that if I could get the entry fee together and persuade someone to drive me, I could go. I then wrote to everyone

I could think of, asking if they could send me money instead of presents for Christmas, as I really wanted to go to this show.

Dad agreed to drive me to Mill Lodge, then left me and Ivan there to stay in the lorry, which was absolutely freezing. It had no living accommodation, so we bunched up the straw in one of the three partitioned areas, then put a blanket down on top of the straw to lie on and we stayed in there without any heater, living on pork pies. But I loved it, it was a great adventure and I was just ecstatic to be there. It didn't matter that the other riders didn't talk to us – we knew we weren't part of that clique, but it was enough for me just to be in their presence and competing alongside the likes of Jonathan Egmore and Jim Edson, even though I was eliminated on most days.

What tickled me pink one day, however, was sitting down to breakfast with some of these top riders, guys I hero-worshipped and tried to emulate. And while I may not have been at the same table as them, sharing the same airspace was good enough for me. I remember Geoff Glazzard being at one table and Mike Saywell at another, the rider who had single-handedly changed the life of this star-struck 15-year-old.

Our family moved to a house called Homeleigh in East Drayton, Retford. It had a nice stable yard and eight acres. Dad had bought it from an old guy and it was a pre-fab, so perhaps not the prettiest house in the world, but Dad transformed it, giving it a complete makeover by covering it with bricks.

Now I can't recall exactly how I managed to cut my hand one Saturday morning – it may have been on a piece of slate that had been lying around after the renovations or on a knife as I was cutting open a bale of hay – but I ended up with a nasty, little gash on my hand. What I do recall, however, is that it was bleeding like hell and that if I'd told anyone about it – which I didn't – I would have had to go to hospital for a couple of stitches. Then they would have bandaged it up and given me an injection, which would have meant no riding the following day and that would have been a disaster. I was going to Kinoulton on the Sunday as there was a Hickstead qualifier, and considering that Sweet Sue and I were doing well, I didn't want to miss the opportunity.

There was nothing for it but to stitch up my hand myself. So I poured some TCP into a saucer, dunked the needle and cotton in it to sterilise them, then stitched up the wound, making two beautiful stitches that any self-respecting doctor would have been proud of! I covered the stitches with a plaster and no one was any the wiser. Then I went to the show, jumped two clear rounds, came second and qualified for Hickstead – easy as that!

The show at Kinoulton was of a slightly lower level than Mill Lodge, which is where I was getting my backside tanned! Kinoulton, on the other hand – even though it was still a qualifying class – was a lot easier, and my success there was a deserved reward for all the time, patience and practice I'd put in with Sweet Sue who was coming on in leaps and bounds. It was like being in a deeper pool and perhaps not swimming as well, but then jumping in the shallow end and finding that you're actually a better swimmer for it. This is a principle I still uphold today – preferring to go to a bigger show and do a little bit better, than staying at a smaller show and win. Confidence is all about realistic goal setting.

What thrilled me about qualifying for Hickstead was the fact I'd got there on my own merits, working my way through problems as I went along. I wasn't having any lessons at this point – what I did do, though, was spend hours poring over my Pony Club manual and any books I could find on showjumping, and learning from my mistakes. Equally, I was delighted that the DIY surgery on my hand was holding up – at least it did for a couple of weeks. Then everything went pear-shaped. I was in an English class showing my friend Wadey – Alastair Wade – my handiwork, but my hand was red and angry looking. It looked as if someone had squeezed a tennis ball under the skin of my palm.

Chapter 6

Wheeling and dealing

- My erupting hand
- Paying the price
- Entrepreneurial ventures
- Leaving school at last

Funnily enough, although my swollen hand looked a sight, it didn't hurt at all. But just to satisfy his own curiosity that I wasn't making it all up, Wadey picked up a pencil and stuck it into my palm as hard as he could. Then I made the biggest mistake and touched it, only gently, and it erupted like Mount Vesuvius all over the desk. Yellow pus cascaded out of the wound like a fountain of thick yogurt, and I yelled and screamed for all I was worth. It hurt, really hurt – and subsequently yogurt has never tasted the same since!

Of course, the English teacher went absolutely mental – more at the disruption I'd caused to his class than at my plight, and he duly dispatched me to hospital telling Wadey that he had to go with me. So together we trundled the two miles to A&E where they attended to my hand.

First, they made a hole, then drained the wound of pus and started to pack the hole with strips of gauze. I had to go to hospital every two or three days to have the gauze changed, whereby they'd cut a new strip about two inches shorter than the previous strip and pack that into the gaping wound. This procedure apparently was to ensure the wound healed in the correct way, from the inside out. This treatment went on for a while.

Needless to say, Mum and Dad were none too pleased with the results of my cack-handed attempts at DIY surgery, for which I more than paid the price. Not only did I become quite ill as a result of good bacteria being eaten up by the copious amounts of penicillin and antibiotics I was given, but I was laid up for a good month. This meant that I missed the Hickstead final I'd qualified for. I was devastated. Not only that, but over the following years, I started to develop a claw hand that was mainly caused by the massive amount of scar tissue which built up in the wound. This created an added problem. Whenever I took a fall, it would result in me breaking my little finger on that hand – more than half a dozen times all told. Luckily, however, this was later repaired in 2000 by an operation in which the joints in that finger were broken and pinned back together. The only evidence of my surgical exploits is a fair amount of external scarring.

Naturally, I was so gutted to have missed the Hickstead final, but the prospect of me leaving school that year was some con-solation. Yet one thing's for sure – I'd never be remembered for my academic brilliance, managing to get only a handful of CSEs. The best grade I mustered was a C in Rural Studies and metalwork. I also scraped through with a C in English. Other subjects were ungraded because coursework was a vital part of the marking – and I didn't do any homework at all! I guess I did well in Rural Studies, because it appealed to me and I was inter-ested in tractors and farming. In fact, Ivan and I both read 'Farmers Weekly' and we'd be able to name various makes of tractor – it was bizarre, because we went from townies to coun-try bumpkins almost overnight. And as we did, the divide between us and the rest of the family became even wider – the elder siblings maintaining their 'townie' roots, while Mum and Dad and us youngsters were becoming more engrossed in coun-try life the more we got involved with the horses.

In fact, Kevin and Iain both moved back to Retford when they got married and Kevin still lives there today. Ivan, on the other hand, went into farming after going to an agricultural college and while he eventually became an Equine Dental Technician, one of the country's best, he doesn't ride anymore, only a motocross motorbike.

The day I left school, I was euphoric – so much so that my final gesture involved me chucking all my school books into the canal on Grove Street on my way home that final Friday. I don't suppose anyone thought too much about that really. It was only to be expected, coming from the lad who was not academic in the slightest. In fact, he was better known for his entrepreneurial ventures and money-making scams than his scholarly prowess. For starters, I had an exceptional reputation as a conker dealer while I was at Freddie's. After all, we had loads of horse chestnut trees near our house in Pinfold Lane, so collecting them and selling them for conker fights seemed too good an opportunity to miss.

After I'd done my pony in the morning, I would go to school with carrier bags full of shiny conkers of all shapes and sizes that I'd carefully selected and divided into freezer bags, securing them with little wire ties. And the bags would all be fastidiously labelled. You could buy bags of natural, oven-baked conkers or ones that even came with the hole already punctured through for the string, and that had been soaked in vinegar and put in the airing cupboard on baking trays to make them go hard. I'd charge 2p for a bag of natural conkers and 5p for the pre-skewered variety as they were more labour intensive.

But what was a conker without a piece of string? I'd already thought of that one. I would offer punters a bootlace at 1p a go and I'd make sure to carry all the paraphernalia required for a conker fight on me. I'd normally have about £1.20-worth of merchandise at any one time and would set up a little stall in the playground, until I was rumbled by the caretaker who put a stop to my little game by reporting me to the 'authorities'. He was an idle so-and-so, and hated having to sweep up after the conker fights, so he made sure my little scam was brought to an abrupt end by telling the headmaster about it.

Any money that I made from selling conkers would be

ploughed back into my 'business' and I'd buy some cigarettes to fund my other entrepreneurial scams. And I had a string of them up my sleeve.

At the time, Swan Vesta matches cost 2p a box and there were 35 matches in a box, while John Player Special cigarettes in the sexy black box cost around 50p for a packet of 20, so ordinarily one cigarette and one match would cost about $2\frac{1}{2}$p. However, I would sell a cigarette and a match for 5p, which was a very healthy profit. That profit increased on windy days, as most of my customers weren't very skilled at lighting up in gale-force winds. I'd stand back, watching and waiting for the wind to blow the match out, then would rush to their rescue offering a replacement match for the bargain price of 1p.

I also used to buy old bikes, do them up and sell them. Clothes, too, were another great seller. At that stage, the mod era fashion was in full swing and everyone – me included – was into drainpipe trousers and bootlace ties. So I'd go to charity shops in search of old shirts with small collars and really narrow ties that I'd sell on at school after Mum had washed them for me. The trousers, too, always needed a good soak, yet it took me ages to realise what they stank of – little old men struggling to get their flies undone in time…

The process of selling has always fascinated me and I loved to be around markets, which I think was the incentive behind all these entrepreneurial tendencies, another of which was my mean line in free-range eggs. After Dad built the stables, the shed that Danny Boy had originally lived in was converted into a hen house in order to house a batch of battery hens a farmer offloaded because they were egg eaters. So we took them on, and Ivan and I designed raised cages with slats so that when the chickens laid their eggs, they'd roll down into a little bed and the chickens wouldn't get the chance to start pecking away at them. And to be doubly sure, we'd fill some of the eggs with mustard which acted as a deterrent – funnily enough, they didn't like the taste.

Our eggs went down well at school, especially with the teachers, as did Ivan's skill at making cricket bats. He fashioned them out of old floorboards with tape wrapped tightly around the handles in the hope that they might look like the real thing. But at only 10p a go, he didn't exactly make his fortune out of them, selling only 15 as everyone obviously decided they were a bit naff.

Of course, all this extra cash came in handy for things we might need to satisfy the usual cravings of adolescent boys, especially ice cream from the van that used to stop outside Freddie's after school. It was fabulous ice cream and the largest tubs they sold cost 22p, which were paid for with the money we'd generate from our respective enterprises. I would go to school every day with not a single penny in my pocket, yet every day I'd make enough money to buy a tub of ice cream, or two.

Aside from buying a few daily essentials, a lot of the money Ivan and I made went into a special fund that I would spend on riding gear and Ivan would spend on bikes. But one of our more notable joint purchases we made was a very flash, if fairly old, DOT scrambler motorbike. DOT (standing for 'Devoid of Trouble') was a famous name in motorcycling from the 1900s to the 1960s, so in today's market it would probably have been quite a sought-after bike. We saved up for months and paid about £70 for it. It had a 250cc engine that was much too big for us, but we loved the bike and we rode it everywhere – sometimes one at a time, sometimes both of us crammed on together. We would race up and down the tracks near the house and in next door's field as fast as it would go, scaring ourselves to death and smashing into the ground if we fell off. Miraculously neither of us suffered any serious injuries as a result.

I was a pretty streetwise teenager and tended to hang out with kids who were a few years older than me, so it was inevitable that I'd try to follow my elders' example. But the sense of maturity, determination, independence and street sense I gained in those formative years had a huge impact on my life, standing me in good stead for the future. I was taught the value of pounds, shillings and pence, as well as the importance of finding the correct marketplace and trying to create a value – be it oven-baked conkers and crappy cricket bats or lorries that required an overhaul or problem horses who needed turning around. In fact, one of my greatest pleasures today is buying and bringing on four-year-olds, educating and producing them to become more of a valuable commodity than they were originally – not just in monetary terms but in ability as well. But I'm nothing if not realistic and if I don't think a particular scheme is going to make me any money, then it's important to reassess and reset the bar, rather than become the patron saint of lost causes.

Chapter 7

He'll never make a rider

- From school to work
- A surprise exit
- Meeting my hero
- Graham Fletcher

Having been a bit of a lost cause at school, I now had the whole world at my feet and it was agreed that I could go to work for a local rider, Tim Fairburn. A friend of mine from the Silver Horseshoe Riding Club, who kept a horse with him, had recommended me for the job. The idea was that I'd work for him for nothing to get a bit of riding experience. I lived in and would go back to see the family and the ponies once a week on my little yellow motorbike with L-plates on the back.

By this time, Marie was riding the ponies back home – she got most of my ponies after me. Aramis, a pony Dad had bought for me from a business colleague, was still on the scene and although we tended to keep each of our ponies a long time, I never got emotionally attached to any of them. This detached attitude was probably due to the fact that, by this stage, I knew what I wanted to do and was getting more competitive. So if a pony wasn't capable of doing the job, I had to move on to another who was.

I started work at Tim Fairburn's yard at 7am one Saturday morning, the very next day after I had ceremoniously dumped everything that reminded me of school into the canal. I was allowed to take my pony with me and the plan was for me to be Tim's second jockey – in other words, his main rider – and train on some of the showjumpers he produced. I got on well with the other people at the yard although, at 15, I was quite a bit younger than most of them. I felt I was really pulling my weight, so while I was at Tim's, I'd applied and been accepted to go onto a Youth Training Scheme, for which I was paid £23.50 a week. Finally I had a few bob in my pocket and it felt great to have a 'wage' coming in. The only dark cloud on the horizon was when Tim found out and wanted £10 for board and lodgings.

Although I learned a lot during the nine months I spent working for him, I was disappointed that the one thing I really wanted to do eluded me. I'd ride my own pony, and then latterly Comedy Star, who I'd purchased through Tim Fairburn from Ann and Chris Wilcox, but I can't remember riding any of Tim's horses, which was one of the reasons I'd gone to work for him. Then out of the blue, Mum rang to say she was coming to pick me up and told me to get my bags packed as she was taking me home. She and Dad arrived within the hour and whisked me and Comedy away, with no explanation for this sudden disappearing act. I was worried that Tim would be angry to find me gone, but all they said was that the arrangement was over. I had no idea why I left Tim Fairburn's yard that day and my parents refused to discuss it with me until a few years later – at the time they just told me it was for the best.

I subsequently found out that unbeknown to me, Mum and Dad had been keeping an eye on the situation, as they were worried about the lack of riding I was doing for Tim. After all, I'd gone for training to be a second jockey. Apparently, they'd had a number of conversations with Tim, asking why I wasn't riding more and he'd told them bluntly that I wasn't good enough.

"I'm not going to ruin my horses by teaching your son to ride," Tim had told them. "I'm not a riding school."

"But how's he going to improve if he's not given the chance to ride?" they'd asked.

"Your son will never be a rider as long as he has a hole in his backside," he reputedly told Mum. That had been the catalyst for whisking me away so quickly. They'd decided not to tell me for fear of crushing my dreams and it probably would have done. I was an impressionable 15-year-old when I started working for Tim and had I known then what I know now, I would have been completely devastated.

When my parents told me about Tim's comment some years after the event, it came as a surprise and I was angry, not just because I was giving him nearly 50% of my earnings but because I'd worked so hard for him and really enjoyed it, in spite of not riding. I thought he was being very hard on me and had I not been going places on Comedy Star, I would have taken it to heart. Even to this day, his damning opinion of my riding ability has stuck with me, although I realise now that his comments were a bit churlish and not important. But it's like a pebble in your pocket – you put your hand in and find it's there, serving as a gentle reminder every now and again. But instead of crawling into a corner and giving up, Tim Fairburn's comments actually gave me a real motivational kick up the backside – a real 'I'll show him' attitude.

Although I felt that Tim was hard on me, I'll admit that I'm sometimes hard on people who work for me or train with me. I'm like that because I had it hard in so many ways, and I think it did me good and made me stronger. You need a shed-load of strength if you're to make it in the horse world. However, I'm also very fair and would never extinguish someone's dream if I could help it. I'll always be honest and realistic, but will never massage people's egos or pamper their ambitions if I don't think they or their horse are going to make the grade. It's not fair on anyone. A lot of people have worked for me and there'll be some folk I've fallen out with, but I hope I've never been unfair to anyone.

These days, I try to be as diplomatic as possible and do my best not to criticise someone's horse or their ambition, but being a bit of a blunt Northerner sometimes gets me into trouble. Years ago, for example, I gave top Italian chef and restaurateur

Aldo Zilli a showjumping lesson, but he wasn't nearly as good a rider as he is a chef.

"Can you cook?" I asked him.

"Of course I can cook," was his retort.

"Great, because you'll never make a living out of riding so I'd stick to the day job if I were you!" Sometimes I just can't help myself. A good few years later, however, who turns up unexpectedly at a horse show in a flash car but the man himself, Aldo.

"That was the best piece of advice anyone could give me, Tim," Aldo shouted to me. "Telling me to stop riding and stick to the day job!"

A sure case of my honesty paying off, I think. More people should be like this, but some find it difficult being honest about their horse's ability, although it's better for owners to realise that their horse might not make it to the top. A case of being cruel to be kind I guess. I know I'm a straight-talking guy, so I try to make sure that everyone around me understands that and then no one is under any illusions. So if people ask my opinion, I tell it to them straight, then there's no confusion or offence taken. Fair enough, they might not always like what I say, but at least they know I've been as truthful as I can.

After my hasty exit from Tim Fairburn's yard, returning home to Homeleigh with its eight acres of land presented new opportunities for me – effectively, the chance to start my own business of sorts at the age of 16. The idea was kick-started by Ann and Chris Wilcox, who I'd met at Tim Fairburn's. Both were respected horse dealers, they liked me and were very supportive, so sent me a couple of youngsters to back at home. While things were slow to get off the ground, it served as a good exercise in learning other aspects of the equestrian industry.

Because I was brave, I started to build up a reputation for being good with tricky horses – those who were nappy or who reared. I remember taking on one particular pony, who'd already been over backwards and broken a wall in the process with his owner, then tried pulling the same stunt with me. He also jumped through a window with me on him. I'd been lying across his back in the stable when he suddenly made a lunge for the open window and jumped clean through it, knocking me off in the process. I was young and stupid so nothing like this fazed me. I would get paid £20 to deliberately 'pull a horse over', which literally involved pulling them over backwards when they reared to frighten them and stop them doing it again – not to be recommended.

Taking on tricky horses wasn't something I wanted to make my living out of, but it was all part and parcel of becoming a good horseman, learning and understanding how they tick and how to put right any problems. It was obviously a case of my past coming back to haunt me and certainly my experience in dealing with my own naughty, nappy ponies was paying off. Sometimes I'd get Mum involved if I needed an extra pair of hands, and she'd follow me through East Drayton in her little blue Mazda. I'd ride these nappy ponies along the roads with Mum behind us, with strict instructions, if it refused to go, for her to jump out of the car and flap a sack behind the pony until it went forward.

The money was trickling in, albeit sporadically, but at least I was doing some riding, although retraining problem ponies wasn't exactly what I'd envisaged. Neither was showing off horses and ponies in Melton Mowbray cattle market. A lot of dealers would take their livestock there and they'd pay me £5 a go to show off their horses to prospective buyers, riding them around the asphalt car park and putting them through their paces as best I could. However, the money would soon mount up, and I could earn £20 to £30 in an afternoon, whereas my brother Kevin – who was working for an architect at the time – was only earning £5 a week. He was definitely in the wrong business.

Although I would rather have been showjumping, these early experiences certainly introduced me to a side of the equestrian industry that I hadn't seen before – the wheeling and dealing, the sharp end of showjumping, and the dealers themselves, who were pretty rough and tough – the tips and tricks they had up their sleeves didn't usually feature in The Pony Club manual.

The jargon they used was pretty loosely defined as well. 'Backed' usually meant that the horse had never had a saddle on in its life. 'Seen hounds' often meant from four fields away and 'sold as seen' usually meant that it was as lame as a dog. But the experience acclimatised me to the nuts and bolts of the industry, and broadened my horizons, giving me the chance to ride horses I may never have had the opportunity to sit on, and there were a few nice ones among the crazy ones. There'd be a few who were cheeky, then there'd be some quality three-year-olds who required backing and bringing on and then there were the downright dangerous ones – I charged extra for those. But the good ones I would produce on myself and get them going nicely for the dealers, after which they'd be sold and I'd make a bit of profit.

This erratic existence was about to change, however, when my showjumping hero, Mike Saywell, moved into the area, to a village called Cottam, a few miles from home. I was so excited when I heard. Mike was still quite a big name in showjumping and on TV, so I didn't waste any time in going round to his house, banging on his door and asking him for a job. I told him that I'd work for nothing; something that I discovered later on had caused a chuckle in the Saywell household. We'd been in Mike's kitchen discussing the job and as I walked out the door, having shaken hands on the deal with the great man, he'd turned and said to his wife Vicky: "I give him a fortnight."

I realised how lucky I was to get this opportunity, so was prepared to do anything on the yard. After all, working for my hero was the stuff that dreams were made of and I wasn't prepared to let it slip through my fingers. It was a fantastic experience just to be around such a professional. And while I was still optimistically searching for that one big break, I realised that I still had to put the work in, serve my 'apprenticeship' and not expect anything to happen for me too soon.

Life at Mike Saywell's yard was to introduce me to new experiences and opportunities. My hours were from 7am-1pm, which still left me time in the afternoon to do my own horses. And I still lived at home, using my motorbike to get me to and from work until I passed my driving test on the morning of my 17th birthday after just two lessons, the equivalent of two hours' driving. I then used Mum's car or would cadge a lift from Dad on his way to work. At Mike's, I would muck out and then ride at least three horses every day. But I would also take it in turn to do the 'breakers', the horses who needed backing, because that meant extra money – a fiver a go. I shared the job with Mike's second jockey, David Moseley, and we kept it fair – him backing one, me backing the next. We would get on anything – even ones who had a bad reputation for turning themselves inside out. But we were both as bad as each other for remembering whose turn it was and an argument frequently broke out.

"I wouldn't get on it for £500," Mike once told us. "And here are you two, squabbling to get on it for a fiver!"

I'm not sure if that showed signs of idiocy or dedication to the job, but as far as I was concerned, it was something that had to be done, a necessary chore. Besides, I loved working for Mike and just wanted to please. As well as being my number one hero for the way he'd won the King George V Gold Cup, he was – and is – a fantastic guy and has been one of the greatest influences in my life. He's a really hard worker and very much a natural horseman, which is why I admire him so much. He doesn't need to use any tricks or weird 'n' wacky ways to get his horses going well for him. If he has an issue, he'll assess the situation coolly and then work through the problem calmly and gradually to a satisfactory conclusion. So not only did I pick up lots at Mike's about riding, I also learnt lots about running a yard and the production of top-class showjumpers.

I hadn't planned on leaving Mike's yard – but about a year later he rang me one day to tell me that Graham Fletcher was looking for a second jockey and that he'd recommended me for the job. He'd apparently put my name forward because he thought it would be a fantastic opportunity for me. I remember being completely stunned when I took the phone call, but managed to gather my wits about me long enough to mutter a "Wow, that's very kind of you, thank you." As much as I was thrilled

and really wanted the job, I was petrified, because Graham –
who was based in Thirsk at this point – was really at the top of
his game and I was still very inexperienced.

Putting my fears aside, however, I went with Mike to the
Doncaster Spring Show and met Graham, an experience that I
will never forget. In fact, I even get nervous thinking about it
today, because I realise now how much the move was to benefit
me. From Mike, it was a fantastic gesture of kindness that turned
out to be a seriously important step up the ladder for me and
one that was to shape my future. But then that's pretty much
how it's been for me all my life – one thing leading to another,
without planning or premeditation, doors opening for me when
I least expected them to. I have been extremely lucky to have
had help and support from so many people, putting me in the
right place at the right time.

I suppose this is largely due to my work ethic, then and now.
I've never fought shy of hard work, especially when it comes to
horses. I realise I'm incredibly lucky to be able to do a job I love
and am reasonably good at. It's more like an extension of a
hobby, I guess. But I've worked long hard hours for it and continue to do so. Many times I've had to work for little or no
money at all, but have always been prepared to do so if it meant
being given a chance to prove myself, even if that did involve
running a few dodgy scams at school to make a few bob! This
life hasn't always been without its risks and challenges, what with
taking on tricky horses and backing belligerent youngsters. But
some risks are worth taking and some opportunities made for
grabbing and I think that that attitude has been paramount to
my success, both in the showjumping arena and other areas of
my business.

I hope this is what Mike saw in me – someone who was willing to accept the long hours, someone prepared to put in the
hard work and someone, even at the tender age of 17, with the
right positive, practical attitude. But then I'm very much a tra-
ditionalist, and I believe in the old-fashioned values of good
manners, hard work, integrity and punctuality. We run a very
professional set-up at home, so when youngsters apply for a job

My first ride – I've ridden a few
donkeys since then! Ivan and me
at Weston-super-Mare

Few people could tell Ivan
and me apart, and we used
to fool them into thinking
I was him and he was me.
Spot the difference

One of our rare holidays abroad – in Monaco. Mum hated flying, so we'd normally holiday in the UK

Proud country boys – the butt of our older brothers' jokes

For all Corky's nappy little ways, he loved his jumping and was one of the bravest ponies I've ever come across. Here we are at Osberton Horse Trials going clear, as usual

Marie and I were keen Pony Clubbers with the Grove – she got most of my ponies after me

Competing at Church Farm near Cannock in 1984, aged 20. I'd like to think my technique has changed a lot since those days. For starters, it helps to look where you're going!

Lye Green Farm in Chesham, Buckinghamshire,
had been an old dairy

I love Border collies and Ben
arrived in a box. He was a
present from Laura and a loyal
companion to the end

Seen here at my desk at Lye Green Farm, I was the captain of industry but it was a
hand-to-mouth existence at times

Supermarket was an unbeatable puissance horse and winning the class at Horse of the Year Show in 1991 put my name on the map

Ex-racehorse Mighty McGuigan had an incredible talent for showjumping that saw him go from novice to Grade A in just nine months

Aboard Toggi Sarlydun Lad with Toggi chairman, the late Philip Billington. I cherished my association with the company because it was my first major sponsorship

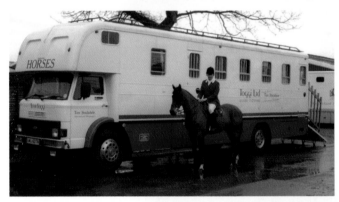

I bought the late Caroline Bradley's wagon – seen here with me on Toggi Interview – when it was sold almost a decade after her death. When I first saw it, there were weeds growing up through the engine, but I restored it to its former glory and even lived in it for six months

Santa's Echo was of Irish breeding and a wilful little character. But for all his quirkiness, he was a prolific winner, picking up eight Grand Prix titles

Toggi Interview tackles the Hickstead Derby Bank. He had a glittering showjumping career

Royal Windsor is one of my favourite shows, no more so than when Her Majesty the Queen is handing out the prizes

We tied the knot on 16 November 1996. Back row, left to right: Geoff Stockdale (my dad), Sian Marta (Laura's best friend and Joseph's godmother), Tim Stockdale, Laura Stockdale, Ivan Stockdale (Laura's dad), Ann Judge (Laura's mum), Andrew Judge (Laura's late stepdad), Tony Cocklin (Laura's dad,) Joy Cocklin (Laura's stepmum). Front row, left to right: Nancy Stockdale (my mum), Robert Buckley, Catherine Buckley (Joy's nephew and niece)

with us, we only consider potential staff members who want to be on our team for the right reasons – not just to work with Tim Stockdale. They must genuinely be prepared for all the hard work that's involved in running a competition yard and be up for making the occasional sacrifice that's inevitable in this business. Working with horses is not a job, it's a vocation, a way of life and if people don't understand that, then they shouldn't be in it.

Having said that, I try to treat everyone who works for me with respect, and ultimately try to be a fair boss to them. I may have the odd rant, because I am a perfectionist and I've got high standards. But if someone proves themself, is a good worker and has talent, then I'll encourage them and there's nothing I wouldn't do to help them achieve what they want from this business. Just as Mike Saywell did for me all those years ago.

Chapter 8

Working for Graham Fletcher

- A new boss
- Making money
- Dumped at Wembley
- Another job interview

Without him even seeing me ride, I got the job with Graham – and, as he later told me, it was on the strength of Mike telling him all about me, on the strength of Mike putting his neck on the line for me and saying I was perfect for the job. I was totally indebted to Mike – still am – and will never forget that act. I'd been working for him for nothing and was obviously something of a useful commodity, but he'd just given me away, not thinking how it might inconvenience him but how it would help me hopefully become a showjumper. Mike hadn't done it because he wanted to get rid of me or because I wasn't being useful – he did it to help me.

There was never any doubt about me taking the job at Graham's. It was obvious that I had to. My heart wasn't really into making a business out of the few horses I had at home to bring on, as I'd had enough of riding horses who spent their life going over backwards. There'd certainly been a lot of frustration brewing at home – rows with my parents, me being a typical teenager I suppose – so Graham's job offer, at £35 a week, couldn't have come at a better time.

Initially, money wasn't the driving force behind my ambition to become a showjumper. It was more important to be competing, getting out there. What I'd been doing so far was at a really low level and I was painfully aware that now, at the age of almost 18, I still hadn't jumped a Foxhunter course. But until this job had come up as Graham's second jockey – his main rider after him – there'd been no opportunity to compete on any of Mike's horses, which is presumably why he'd put me up for this job with Graham. All things considered, I was lucky to get taken on by Graham, because I was totally under-qualified for it. Second jockey to Graham Fletcher, but without a single Foxhunter under my belt? It was all pretty serious stuff by then, with Graham sponsored by Team Schneider, the hi-fi giants.

During the 16 months or so that I was with Graham, I grew up tremendously. I was a long way from home, so life for me took on a different meaning and I learned to fend for myself. And while it sounded quite grand to say I was living in my own staff cottage, there was the little matter of the daily household chores that came with it – the rigmarole of cooking, cleaning and washing my own clothes. Working for Mike Saywell, I'd still been living at home so Mum was doing an awful lot for me, but now I had to stand on my own two feet and learn how to do these things for myself. I didn't have a lot of stuff to worry about, though – a pair of shoes, my riding boots, a pair of trousers, pair of jeans and a couple of shirts in case I needed to be seen in public. Even when I met Laura at the age of 27, all I had to my name was my clothes, a bed, duvet and a television.

As far as food was concerned, my culinary skills weren't really put to the test and I resorted to lots of takeaway stuff, although I did cook up a mean Fray Bentos steak and ale pie or frozen mince pancake. Other than that, I lived on toast and cereal, usually Frosties or Sugar Puffs, and chocolate, Galaxy and Cadbury's Creme Eggs being particular favourites. I was never keen on vegetables and the nearest I got to any fruit was the occasional glass of orange juice.

Unsurprisingly then, there wasn't a lot of meat on me in those days – in fact, I was unbelievably thin and my nickname at

Graham's was Stick, because I had legs like matchsticks. Nevertheless, my lean frame belied my capacity for being able to hold my drink and I could knock back whisky like it was going out of fashion.

It had been a night out, something new for me having just left home, and there'd been a comedy show at 'Billingham Big Night Out' – hosted by the comedian Bernard Manning. It was on this occasion that I met Robert and Steven Smith for the first time and it turned out to be a night memorable for its laughter, stories, male bonding, general camaraderie and the fact that I sank 23 double Scotches to become the whisky drinking champion, something that still gets talked about today.

Sensibly, we'd ordered a minibus to take us all home that evening but thinking the driver had gone past my stop, I jumped up into the aisle and shouted to him to stop. As he hit the brakes, I was catapulted from one end of the minibus to the other straight into the windscreen. I don't remember much about the incident, but obviously managed to pick myself up and stagger to the front door of my house because I woke next morning propped up against the door. I must have tried to put my key in the lock, failed miserably, then given up and slumped to the floor in a heap to sleep in one of my nice shirts.

Even to this day, I'm occasionally reminded by Robert of the night I met the Smith brothers and recalled as the thin, big-eared, spotty lad who could drink a lot of whisky. Big nights out were, however, few and far between but it was part and parcel of the job that you ended most days with a pint down the pub.

Obviously a busy yard, the hours at Graham's were long and hard, so I had to be committed from the start. Graham owned a horse called Cool Customer, one of his top horses, and here I was, given him to ride. By that point, everyone's favourite, Buttevant Boy, had just retired but he was still in a field down at Sowerby, so I used to feed and look after him. I remember being proud of this job, because I knew how much he meant to Graham.

It was at Graham's that I first qualified for Horse of the Year Show on a horse called Barolo, owned by Larry Burrell.

Graham didn't gel with him straightaway but I did, to the extent that I beat Graham in the qualifier. It was a time of mixed emotions for me. On one hand, I was thrilled, but on the other, I felt really guilty about beating my boss. I remember us driving the horses home together and Graham was fuming. We drove through the gates and as he got out of the lorry, he turned to me and said: "Of all the days to go well, you have to choose this one." And with that, he stormed off. This was obviously his competitive mindset coming out.

But he soon got over his disappointment and actually fought for me to keep the ride when Larry Burrell said he wanted Graham to continue riding the horse. Graham was having none of it and said that because he didn't qualify the horse, he wasn't going to ride it in the final at Horse of the Year Show. Knowing that Graham was behind me at that stage in my career, obviously believing I was worthy of the ride, did my confidence a power of good. As it turned out, this was just one of many incidences when Graham fought my corner. I felt indebted to him and soon began to realise that, under that sometimes serious temper of his, he was actually a very fair man.

But for all the competition experience I was gaining – usually taking a couple of horses to little county shows where I'd often win the Open and scoop the £50 prize – there was still the matter of money and my determination to make a decent wage. It was then, therefore, that I started to put in some extra hours on the Fletcher farm, run by Graham's parents. They offered me work hoeing sugar beet, essentially turning over the soil between the rows of sugar beet. But while the wages were good at £4 an hour, the work was gruelling, resulting in excruciating blisters, and the hours were long and tedious. I'd hoe beet from 4-7am, work for Graham from 7am-6pm, be back on the beet from 6-10pm, and then be up again at 4am. I only did it for a few weeks, but the funds were welcome. Life for me, however, was soon about to change. One evening when Graham got back from Leicester County Show, he called in at my staff cottage in Carlton Miniott, something he rarely did.

He suggested we go for a pint at the local pub, The Dog and

Gun, and he told me that a local owner-breeder (John) 'Jet' Taylor needed a new rider for his 50-odd horses. Apparently, he had a fantastic place in Leicester and Graham thought it might be a good move for me. Of course, I was immediately on the back foot thinking that I'd done something wrong and that Graham was trying to get rid of me. On the contrary – just as Mike Saywell had done, Graham was trying to help me out. Try as he might to convince me it was an opportunity too good to miss, he could sense my reticence. Graham knew I loved working for him and I was adamant I wasn't going to go. So thanks, but no thanks, I told him, I was staying put. Perhaps it had been a knee-jerk reaction on my part, but I wasn't going to make any hasty decisions. I needed time to think things through and that's exactly what I did that evening when I got back from the pub. I turned the idea over and over in my head. Maybe it was a good idea, after all, I contemplated as I lay awake tossing and turning, worrying that I may have made the wrong decision.

What made me knock on Graham's door at 9am the next day, I'll never know, but there was something niggling in the back of my mind. Opportunities like this don't come along every day and I respected Graham's opinion and experience, so I told him that I'd changed my mind and that I would like to talk to Jet. He managed to convince me that while I was a good, little worker and that he really didn't want to lose me, the chance to be Jet's first jockey was the next rung up the showjumping ladder. What's more, Jet had had a few big names riding for him – such as Mike Saywell and Malcolm Pyrah. He enjoyed considerable success with some of his horses, like Uncle Max, ridden by Ted Edgar and Seven Valleys, ridden by Johan Heins. I decided that if I could emulate just a fraction of their success, I'd be thrilled.

So it was that I went for my interview with Jet – I was just about 18 at this stage – and I remember being completely bowled over by his incredible set-up. The yard was brand new and immaculate, and there were horses as far as the eye could see – everything from youngsters ready to be backed to Grade A showjumpers, and he wanted someone to ride and compete them. And that someone was going to be me.

My living accommodation was a lovely, three-bedroomed house that I would share with Jet's other staff and I was given my own transport, a blue Toyota Hilux pick-up truck. I thought I'd died and gone to heaven – I couldn't believe this was happening to me. This was big-time stuff – I'd arrived and just couldn't stop smiling to myself. Later that day, I didn't just drive back to Yorkshire, I floated, and my first port of call was to see Graham to thank him for everything. He had done me a huge favour.

Mind you, this tends to happen a lot in showjumping, when you have someone on your yard who has worked hard, been reliable and is a good jockey. Of course you'd like them to stay but it's only natural that you want to help them out if you can. I always feel a certain amount of pride when I hear that past staff members are doing well and there's a bit of me that hopes Mike and Graham feel the same about me. I can never repay them for the opportunities they gave me – I wouldn't even know where to start, other than to say there is nothing I wouldn't do for either of them.

It reminds me of a time when we invited a teenager to do some work experience with us. We knew the family and their son, who was keen to be a showjumper. He was a cracking little rider, and really keen and willing at first. We involved him in everything on the yard and he was fitting in really well, then it suddenly went belly up. About a week into the arrangement, his mum came to pick him up – just as mine had done at Tim Fairburn's yard, except that I definitely hadn't told the mum that her son couldn't ride, as Tim had said to mine. On the contrary, he could ride – and very well. But this lad had decided that he wanted to go back to ride his ponies at home.

His mum wasn't sure whether or not he'd be back – and he wasn't. He just disappeared without a by your leave, nor a single word of thanks, and that was the last we saw of him. It left me puzzled. Here was a good example of someone being handed a great opportunity on a plate, not realising its worth and chucking it all away. What really rankled with me, though, was not so much the disappearing act and the wasted opportunity for him, but the chance denied to someone else.

Jet Taylor, however, was a different kettle of fish altogether. I found him to be a hard taskmaster, a difficult man to work for and an obstinate so-and-so. He made the rules and you lived by them, or you'd be out of a job before you knew where you were. I lasted 11 months with him, but I knew of staff who'd reported for their first day's work in the morning and who'd left by the afternoon.

My time at Jet's didn't get off to a very good start. I was given six youngsters to ride on my first afternoon, some of which had never had a rider on their back, but it was my job to back them and I thought that by the fifth one, I was doing pretty well. There'd been no mishaps and everything had gone as well as could be expected until the very last horse. He threw his head right back, smacked me clean in the face and broke my nose. I was covered in blood, but despite that, it had been a reasonably good day and I felt happy with the way it had gone. But Jet was not a man for praise or encouragement and things continued in much the same vein, with Jet wielding his authority like the tough man he was. He was a man of great principle and would stand for no nonsense.

We'd been down to Wembley for the day to watch some Horse of the Year Show classes and had had a good day meeting people and watching the horses. Then at the end of the day, he told me that he wanted me ready to leave for home "at 10 o'clock, mate". He called everyone mate. So at the witching hour, I left the bar where I'd been having a few jars, just in time to see his car – a Mercedes with his personalised JET 192 (standing for John Edward Taylor) numberplate – moving off without me. I ran after him, yelling and whistling to attract his attention, and was amazed that he couldn't hear me. Either he genuinely couldn't or he had decided to ignore me, which was probably more than likely. I watched as the red tail-lights disappeared from view. He'd left me in London. I was not yet 18, didn't even have a jacket and had about £2.60 in my pocket.

Luckily, however, a national coach company took pity on me after I told them I'd been dumped and they let me get on a coach going to Lutterworth, which isn't far from Leicester – about 15 miles. It was a slow journey back, though, and we pulled in to Lutterworth at about 2am, but there was still the matter of the walk back home and I remember falling in through the front door at about 6.30am, just half-an-hour before I was due on the yard – just in time for a confrontation with Jet. But there was no apology from him and he showed no remorse for leaving me.

"Time's time, mate," he said. "You weren't there, you were late. Time's time."

Jet did a similar thing to me when we went to a show in Nuneaton. I couldn't drive the big lorry that took six horses, so he had to come with me and the plan was to leave at 9am. I'd made sure I was up early that morning to feed and groom the horses, and load them onto the lorry before going inside to get myself ready – have a wash, shave and change into my riding gear. And as I was getting ready – I was running fractionally late – I heard the engine roar into life and ran to the window to see what was going on. Jet was only leaving without me again! I couldn't believe it and this time, rather than be flabbergasted as I had been at Wembley, I was furious. I ran out, hollering after him, but it was all to no avail as I watched the lorry disappear around the corner. There was nothing for it than to follow him to the show in my pick-up.

"You went without me again," I yelled at him when I arrived at the showground. "I've done all the horses this morning, groomed them, got all their equipment together and then you disappear without me."

"Time's time," he replied infuriatingly.

The thing is, I knew that he could do what he wanted. I had been late. There was no give and take with him, no discussion, everything was black or white, he called the shots and if you didn't like it, you could lump it. And he wouldn't have batted an eyelid if I hadn't chased after him in my pick-up. As he reminded me, there were plenty of riders who would have willingly ridden his horses for him that day and he was right.

Now, being able to reflect on those tough times and taking on all sorts of jobs to make ends meet, I suppose I can see where Jet was coming from. Everything had to be just so – after all, he was the governor and it was his business that he was running. So, as harsh as all these knocks and setbacks may sound now, they were all part of the learning curve and they were events that would shape my career and define my ability to run my business as I do today. And believe me, it isn't just about riding horses for a living: it's about all the other behind-the-scenes aspects involved in running a successful competition and training yard.

I had my 18th birthday while I was working for Jet and we had a little do in the pub. Impetuously, I had got engaged to my first serious girlfriend by this point, Caroline Harcombe, a groom who had worked for Graham Fletcher for a short time. She'd followed me down to a job in Leicester, but the relationship just added to my frustrations at that time – I felt as if I was going nowhere. I was too young to rationalise the serious aspects of life – an engagement and the commitment to be together forever being just one of many. Looking back, I was much too young to get engaged and I probably made the commitment because it seemed like a good idea at the time. I obviously didn't think it through properly, but it made me realise that you have to do these things for the right reason – and I didn't have one at the time. But in the end, the relationship just fizzled out like a damp squib.

I'd been riding a couple of horses who'd both gone lame and had reached their sell-by dates – namely, Smittee and Proper Job. I was also riding a lovely mare called Jet Run, who was going to be a good 'un. But the final straw came the day Jet decided to sell her. "That's my showjumping career you've just sold," I cursed him under my breath.

Then as luck would have it, one Thursday when I bought my copy of 'Horse & Hound', there was an interesting-sounding advertisement for a groom/rider, with the possibility of competing. And this was to be yet another of those spontaneous out-of-the-blue turning points. So I applied for the job and contacted one Susan Meyerding – or 'Merryding' as I called her – and off I went, in search of new beginnings.

Susan lived in Flaunden, near Hemel Hempstead, Hertfordshire, with her husband Lutz, a banker. Their place was immaculate, like something I'd never seen before. It was a beautiful courtyard-style yard and there was a pretty little two-bedroomed cottage that went with the job, situated down a bit from the main house. They had a private yard filled with Susan's own horses – five of them, all showjumpers. The idea was that they wanted someone to help with the usual stuff around the yard and do a bit of riding. So they invited me for an interview and I travelled south from Leicester, again full of hope and expectation that this might at long last be the chance to really show people what I was capable of. I was beginning to think that I was never going to get my big break, but I had a good feeling about this job. Only time would tell.

Chapter 9

Hitting the international scene

- Opportunity knocks
- Angeac-Champagne – my first international show
- Steak bravo!
- Called for the Nations Cup

I was excited and nervous at the prospect of a new job as I drove down to Hemel Hempstead from Leicester. Excited because I had a good feeling about it. At Jet's yard, there were no horses for me to compete on and I didn't feel I was progressing in any way. It was, therefore, a matter of grabbing every opportunity that presented itself.

I felt the nervous excitement anyone would experience if they thought they could be on the verge of a life-changing move at the age of 19. However, any nervous anticipation I had was quickly dispelled when I met Susan and Lutz Meyerding – they were lovely, friendly and very welcoming. There'd be five horses to look after on their yard, with just me and Susan doing the riding. She was going to do three and I would get two – Ragged Robin and Supermarket. They'd been beautifully schooled by my predecessor, the eventer Julian Trevor-Roper, brother of Mary-Anne Trevor-Roper, who was one of the trainers who worked with me on Channel 4's 'Faking It' and the BBC's 'Only Fools on Horses' TV programmes.

Anyway, here I was being handed these two magnificent

horses on a plate. To say I was excited about the job was an understatement, mainly because Supermarket had recently come second in a big international class at Towerlands. I couldn't help daydreaming that, maybe one day, I'd be able to compete him as well. The interview went smoothly and they gave me the job, right there and then.

I loved working for Susan and Lutz. They must have felt fond of me because I proudly became godfather to one of their daughters, Victoria. They were kind, keen and passionate about the sport. What's more, they were knowledgeable, had a good reputation and tended to leave me to my own devices as far as Ragged Robin and Supermarket were concerned. I got on very well with the two horses and did a few of the bigger national circuit shows with them, before moving on to competing in the top classes at county shows. While Ragged Robin was doing really well, Supermarket was something special and rocketed straight to Grade A in just one season. Obviously the hard work was paying off and we were starting to get known around the national circuit. On the strength of this, I was asked by other owners to ride their horses.

Things were starting to snowball for me after a few good results and my head was in a bit of a spin. I was beginning to get a real buzz out of riding and a sense of optimism the likes of which I'd never experienced before. I've never been one to count my chickens, but surrounded by all these wonderful horses and supportive owners, it was difficult not to. Especially when I received a chance phone call from one John Cosgrove. He'd phoned the yard wanting to talk to a Tim Price.

"I'm terribly sorry," I said, "you must have been given the wrong number – I'm Tim Stockdale."

"Do you do showjumping lessons?" John asked.

"Yes, I do, but there's also a trainer called Tim Price," I'd replied.

"No, you'll do," said John, "you're the man I need. I'd like to book some lessons for me and my daughter."

John and his daughter, Lauren, would pitch up for a lesson every Tuesday at 7pm, and sometimes his son Alex would come along, too. They'd always turn up late in a rickety, old, red Bedford TK lorry, out of which they'd drag their scruffy ponies and there'd always be a kerfuffle, accompanied by plenty of yelling and screaming. It was mayhem. Alex would usually ride in a pair of old hunting boots and invariably forget his hat.

"I'm going to call you Charles," I announced to him one day.

"Why's that?" he asked.

"Because you're Charles Atlas, as in hat-less!" I chuckled. I still call him Atlas now.

For all John's casual, laid-back approach – 6ft 4in of him in skin-tight breeches, tired-looking leather boots and unruly, curly hair – I remember liking him right from the word go. He was, and is, a very friendly, warm, open guy, a really normal person with no side to him, and I really enjoyed teaching him and Lauren. We'd pass the time of day talking about anything and everything, although the main subject was naturally horses. And he was always polite in enquiring how business was going.

Then one day, I told him about showjumper Robert Bell's horses, which were at our yard. Lutz had leased them for me to ride but with the idea they'd be sold on. We'd been going really well on the circuit – one of the horses, Loctite Aries, had won four classes in a row. On the strength of that, someone was coming to have a look with a view to buying him. I was a bit miffed really, because I'd put a lot of effort into him when he came to our yard. But for all his carefulness and unbelievable talent, Aries was quite a quirky horse, because he would never jump water. Instead, he would canter straight through it and no matter what the rider did, he was having none of it. So in a speed class, you knew that at least four seconds would be added, as it was then, so you'd have to step on the gas to make up for time elsewhere. However, this was obviously not reason enough to dissuade potential buyers. John could sense my mood and enquired how much the horse was on the market for.

"£18,000," I told him.

"I'll buy him for you," he replied casually. Of course I thought he was joking. Only at the end of the lesson when John mentioned it again did I realise he was, in fact, deadly serious. I was flabbergasted. I had no idea what John did for a living and didn't think it was my place to ask – I'd always assumed he was just a 'normal guy' and that he'd tell me if he wanted to.

One thing I did know about John, though, was that he was a keen sportsman. At the time, I was playing in a squash league at a club in London Colney, just outside St Albans, so one day we decided to have a game. We arranged to meet at John's house in Chalfont St Peter, Buckinghamshire, an area I didn't know at all, and then we'd drive from there. So he gave me directions to his house and they took me down a long, winding driveway, at the end of which was an enormous manor house called The Gate House. As I swung into the drive, an Alsatian came running over to my little Fiat Strada, barking and growling for all he was worth. Deciding I was obviously in the wrong place, I high-tailed it out of there, being careful not to ding the Range Rover and Porsche as I turned my car around. Eventually, I found a phone box and rang John.

"I followed your directions," I told him, "but came to an enormous white house with a fierce Alsatian patrolling the grounds."

"Sounds about right," he replied.

So assuming John must be the gardener or handyman to the owners of the house, I retraced my steps, arrived and cautiously got out of the car, one eye looking out for the Alsatian, and rang the doorbell. Seconds later, John came to the door and invited me in to have a look around. It was a beautiful house – I'd never seen anything like it and whoever lived there must have been worth a bob or two, I thought at the time. I mean, it had everything, including the obligatory swimming pool.

"This is magnificent, John," I said, "but the owner won't mind you showing me around, will he?" I asked slightly anxiously, as I didn't want John to get into any trouble.

"No worries there, Tim, that shouldn't be a problem. Because I am the owner!"

I was gobsmacked and remember driving with John in stunned silence to the squash club. I'd been teaching him and his family to ride for two years, but hadn't known that he was a very successful property developer. I remember recoiling with embarrassment as I replayed some of the conversations I'd had with him, criticising southerners for being unfriendly in the pubs, unlike in Yorkshire where everyone says 'goodnight' as you leave. I'd told him how much I hated working down south and that if it wasn't for the kindness and support of Susan and Lutz, I'd have gone back up north ages ago. I'd slammed the southerners for all having Volvos and swimming pools... And here he was with his pool and flash cars. I felt a complete berk.

But the Cosgroves stuck with me and kept coming for lessons. They are still with me today but in a different capacity, as they own and keep two horses with me – Fresh Direct K2 (aka Big) and Abelardo EZ (aka Eze). In fact John, who has become a loyal family friend, has had a huge impact on my life, past and present, and has always been there for me and Laura if we've needed advice or someone to mull things over with.

I remember he came with us to have a look at Dovecote Farm when we first thought of buying it; and he made sure the Channel 4 documentary I did years ago, 'Cutting Edge', was right for me. He really is a lovely guy, genuine through and through, and phones every week for a chat. John charms everybody he meets and is one of life's good people – if only there were more like him. He's always been there for me if I needed any advice and we've never had a cross word, even though he's a staunch supporter of Arsenal Football Club – but then there's no accounting for taste. What I love about John is that although he has done extremely well for himself, he's not flash with his cash but very much down to earth. All in all, I'm lucky to have some fantastic owners and John and Janet Cosgrove are two of them.

Susan and Lutz Meyerding also continued to feature heavily in my early career, giving me chance after chance to prove myself on some amazing horses. My name was getting out there and becoming known on the county circuit, which was almost the equivalent of serving an apprenticeship. Equally, John Cosgrove was becoming a very influential supporter and pivotal component in my life, effectively affording me the opportunity to gain some experience at the next level by buying Loctite Aries for me. While Aries was proving to be worth his weight in gold (in spite of his water phobia) and Ragged Robin had gone to Grade A with me, it was Supermarket bringing home the bacon and the horse I was to ride at my first European competition.

Travelling to my first full-blown international show on the Continent was a totally different ball game for me and it was difficult to contain my excitement and pride. Excitement because I felt that this was the opportunity I'd been waiting for, and here were two people, Susan and Lutz, not only entrusting me with their prized horses, but also putting their necks on the line and believing in me. Pride, because I'd be representing my country, something that still gives me a buzz today. And believe me, there are few things in life these days that evoke as much emotion in me as a podium place, with the Union Jack flying aloft and the National Anthem playing. It still gets me choked, even after all these years. Let's not forget either that I was still only in my early twenties, so the weight of responsibility bore heavy on my young, inexperienced (and still skinny) shoulders.

Travelling to France in Susan's lorry was something else and I couldn't stop smiling to myself as we trucked along to our destination in Angeac-Champagne, near the town of Cognac in the Bordeaux region, with Supermarket safely stowed in the back. What made the whole experience even sweeter was that we'd been formally invited to the show, something that happened a lot in those days, and when Susan and I arrived at the showground, I couldn't believe my eyes. You could be forgiven for thinking that this was someone's very large back garden, with its own arena and a pretty, ornamental bridge spanning a gently trickling stream – it was like Eden, with its expanse of neatly manicured lawns and superb stabling and facilities for the horses. It was beautiful and I remember thinking that if all shows on the Continent were like this, then I'd be spending most of my time over here. I could quite happily get used to this.

What's more, our hosts were generous. Each evening, there'd be a reception for the riders, which presented the perfect opportunity for me to get to know my fellow competitors, not least two great guys with whom I've remained firm friends to this day – German rider Alois Pollmann-Schweckhorst and Frenchman Robert Breul. I suppose the common denominator for all of us was that this was our first-ever international show, and it formed the tie that cemented our friendship.

While it was a real honour to be invited to this wonderful show, I almost felt guilty at taking their money, for not only were they looking after us well, they also paid us an appearance fee, not unusual in those days. Today, of course, you have to pay to enter and cover the cost of any corporate box you may want to hire for sponsors and guests. The French hosts also financed our board and lodging, but I decided to live in the lorry for the few days I was there and put the 'housekeeping' towards the cost of my entry fees and diesel. This, as it happens, was a good move.

Memorable though the event had been, Lady Luck hadn't been on my side and I managed just a fourth place on the last day in the last class, for which I received a plaque of which I was immensely proud.

So, I left France glowing with the memory of my first international show, even though I now realised I'd made a bit of a faux pas at the first official function in Angeac-Champagne. I couldn't believe my luck when I'd studied the menu – steak and chips. However, the steak they were serving that night was incredibly rare – much too rare for me – so I wanted to ask for one that was well done, but my French at that stage was practically non-existent. I dug deep in the memory banks hoping that I might be able to dredge the words up from the dim and distant past, but nothing sprang to mind. I was wracking my brains scrambling around for the words, but it was no good, I was completely sunk. And then it dawned on me... Why hadn't I thought of this before? So proudly I asked for a 'steak bravo', because all I'd heard when any of us had performed well was 'bravo', as in 'well done'. So there it was, quite simply and quite sensibly I thought... A steak bravo!

My second international show was also in France – in Dunkerque later that year – but it couldn't have been more different. The whole experience was in stark contrast to the glitz and glamour of my first visit to the Continent and memorable because it was everything that beautiful Angeac-Champagne was not – very poor show arrangements and dire accommodation in a really smelly guesthouse. It was a real eye opener for me, but in hindsight summed up international showjumping to a 'T' – one minute you're living the high life with the sun shining and the champagne flowing, the next you're being brought down to earth with a bump, making do in the grottiest place ever! So while Dunkerque itself didn't exactly do it for me and was quite forgettable, the memory of meeting French showjumper Eric Navet for the first time is as clear as a bell – but for all the right reasons. He made me laugh.

While I could regale you with stories of Eric starting to make it big on the showjumping scene – which he was – and although he was a tall, very elegant, long-legged rider, what I remember him for was the size of his feet. They were massive and not helped by the big, baggy boots he wore that looked like wellies, not like my skinny, tight-fitting ones. They were the source of great amusement to me and I remember thinking they looked ridiculous. The more I told myself not to stare at them, the more I had to. But Eric had a great sense of humour and took it all in his stride. He's obviously forgiven me for the jokes and jibes about his humongous feet, because we have a very good friendship now.

Eric was a very consistent rider who was placed in a lot of competitions at Dunkerque that year, although I did pretty well too. In the puissance I took a third or fourth place. But I didn't do another puissance class for a while after that, but I was lucky enough to return to Angeac-Champagne with Supermarket the following year when I was invited back for a second time. I'd written a thank-you letter to the organisers after my first visit, saying how much I enjoyed competing there and how I'd love to go back at some stage, so when I received the invitation to return, I was thrilled. Again, there was no expense spared and we were all really well looked after, with lavish dinner parties every evening and the chance to meet and mingle with more new kids on the showjumping block. This time, I got talking to Dutch-born rider Rob Hoekstra.

Angeac-Champagne was probably one of Rob's first international shows. Today, however, he features fairly prominently in my life as Team GBR's Chef d'Equipe. He moved to England from Holland with his parents in the late Seventies and took up British nationality in 1987. Rob trained with Dutch rider Albert Voorn, was an impressive showjumper as a youngster, had represented Holland on the Junior Showjumping team and was winner of the Hickstead Derby. He has also represented Great Britain on a number of Nations Cup teams. These days, though, Rob's main focus is on training and he has worked with international riders at European, Olympic and World level.

I liked competing in France, because everything was very civilised and organised. It's one country that seemed to draw me to competitions like a magnet, then and now. What's more, my horses felt happy there and more often than not went well for me. The French seemed to like me which was good news – probably because I was getting a bit of consistency on the county and national circuit in the UK and, more importantly, a reputation for winning. Invitations to compete on the Continent – mainly France – started to flood in. I was excited, thrilled and honoured, especially when asked to compete in a friendly match between France and England in Nantes.

The show was held slap bang in the centre of town, in the main square on a sort of ash and sand-type arena. It was like nothing I'd jumped on before, I liked it and the horse I was riding that day – a new mare belonging to the Meyerdings called Newmarket – seemed happy enough with it, or so I thought. She was quite sharp and feisty, and I suppose what you'd call a typical mare, as in you can 'tell' a gelding but must 'ask' a mare. But attitudes aside, she had a big jump in her and I never got the feeling she'd ever throw in a dirty stop.

We'd decided to enter Newmarket into a particular class, a speed class, on the first day of the show and it all seemed to be going well. The mare was on her toes, and I felt relaxed and confident. The course was testing, but there was nothing I was particularly worried about until we made what was a really sharp turn between two fences, having jumped a huge parallel that I thought we'd handled pretty well. But as I was looking towards the next fence, I felt her pull to the fence that we were turning inside – in other words, she was heading for the wrong jump and I had no alternative but to give her a tug to redirect her. Too late, though, she was on it, but realising that she had nowhere to go and was too close to take off, she stopped dead in her tracks and threw her head clean up into mine, smacking me right in the face. There was an almighty crack as my jaw took the full impact of the blow and I can't even remember falling off. She'd knocked me out cold.

The next thing I realised as I came to was that there was a group of people huddled around me, none of whom I knew, but who were all staring down with anxious, horrified looks on their faces – 'I'm not that ugly,' I thought. There was a lot of frenetic activity as everyone rushed around shouting in French, not a lot of which I understood at the time, although my French isn't that bad now. The only sign that my injury might be serious and warrant medical attention was when a strange French guy tried sticking his hand down my throat. It turned out that he was actually Dr Philippe Olieric, the President of the show – and a respected medic. He thought I had swallowed my tongue.

Although I was a bit doolally, I can still remember the pain as if it were yesterday – it was excruciating, unbelievable pain, the like of which I'd never experienced before and hoped never to again. Still, here I was with some Frenchman – who's now a very good friend of the family – trying to grapple my tongue from the back of my throat. At one point, as the pain gripped my body even more, I whacked him right on the side of the head. It was the only way I knew how to attract this guy's attention, as I obviously couldn't speak with his hand shoved down my throat. I punched him so hard on the side of the head that he looked as if he'd just gone 10 rounds with Mike Tyson.

I was taken off to the local infirmary where they diagnosed that my jaw was fractured in two places. The doctor alerted Susan, who wasted no time in contacting a plastic surgeon living just down the road from her yard in Flaunden. He told her that while I could probably cope as I was for the time being, I'd need the jaw wired up so arranged to do that as soon as I got home. But I had to get back first and that meant driving the lorry home with a broken jaw. Although I was in complete agony, I couldn't help but laugh, for two black lines had developed down either side of my face where the fractures were. It looked as if someone had drawn on two perfectly symmetrical lines with a black Biro – I looked a right sight, a bit like Dr Frankenstein's monster.

As soon as I got home to the yard in Flaunden, I was admitted to the Clementine Churchill Hospital in Harrow, Middlesex. I was operated on under local anaesthetic so that I wouldn't have to be kept in overnight and they wired my jaw shut. Then three days later, I rode at Hillingdon in the Area International Trial and won it, complete with busted jaw.

Susan, however, had to sit at the side of the ring and be ready to spring into action with a set of wire cutters, just in case I fell off, vomited and choked. And although the rule about wearing hats with chinstraps had just come into being, I was given special dispensation not to wear mine, as a strap digging into the jaw was just too painful, so I got away with wearing my favourite Beagler. That victory more than compensated for all the agony, discomfort and inconvenience of not being able to talk – a relief, some would say. However, the fact that I couldn't brush my teeth for three weeks and had to live on liquidised food during that time, sucking it through a straw, did nothing to raise my spirits.

Even after the drama in Nantes, the British team selectors must have thought I was cutting the mustard on the international scene because I finally received 'the call', the summons that said I'd been picked for my first Nations Cup in 1988 at the age of 24. It was to be held in Bratislava which could have been anywhere for all I knew. But I discovered that it was in the former Czechoslovakia (now Slovakia). It seemed like the end of the earth because it was so far away from home. I needn't have worried, though, because I was travelling with the rest of the team – Andy Austin, Paul Sutton and James Fisher, who were all roughly the same age as me and are still my buddies today. Because it was such a long way to go, we had planned to break the journey with a few other shows along the way and this is when I began to discover what this international life on the road was really like.

Chapter 10

Lads on tour

- Youthful optimism
- The never-ending journey
- A pain in the backside
- Welcome to Czechoslovakia

If I thought I'd been excited at the prospect of taking part in my first international, then I certainly wasn't prepared for the gamut of emotions that engulfed me at the thought of competing on the British team in my first Nations Cup in 1988 – the responsibility was huge and there were so many people gunning for us and relying on us to perform well for our country. It was pressured – no doubt about that – but I discovered that this was something I could handle pretty well and actually enjoy. Showjumping is an adrenaline-fuelled business and I seemed to thrive on the pressure.

Setting off with three other likely lads – Andy Austin, Paul Sutton and James Fisher – on our biggest showjumping adventure yet was a thrill. All eyes would be upon us, but maybe not always for the right reason.

Preparing for this long-haul journey was something new to me. I sure as hell knew how to pack a lorry, although what we'd take then is not a patch on what we'd pack today. In those early days, I'd take just a tack trunk about 3ft 6in x 4ft 6in which would hold everything. These days, however, we take enough to fill a two-horse trailer packed to the gunnels – everything from the obvious tack, boots and rugs to an ice machine goes on the inventory. On top of that, there's all the veterinary stuff – magnetic rugs, lotions, potions, vitamins, electrolytes and supplements, plus feed, hay and bedding.

And not forgetting my riding gear – two jackets, two hats, two pairs of boots, 12 sets of spurs of different lengths, two pairs of gloves and three whips of differing lengths. Then, in the ring bag which my groom takes care of, there's a bottle of water, Polos, a spare flash strap, hole punch, insulation and gaffer tape, string, buttons and chewing gum.

All this equipment would be enough for three horses over a weekend and while taking this little lot is all very well and good when we drive to the Continent, if we fly further afield, that list gets stripped down considerably, but then we'd probably only take two horses. In that situation, we wouldn't take spares of everything, but join forces with the other riders as far as the bigger items were concerned. One thing's for sure, though – it's all essential kit. If there's one thing I am, it's a stickler for detail and preparation which is so important at a competition – there has to be some semblance of routine to ensure that everything runs smoothly and without incident.

So here we were, all packed and ready to embark on the biggest test yet. It was a huge adventure setting off with two big wagons and several tons of very valuable horseflesh. As we trucked our way through Europe, all we needed were a couple of CB radios and a few Yorkie bars. But there was one thing niggling me and that was how nervous I felt about the length of the journey. At the same time, it seemed ridiculous to drive all that way just for one show. In those days, the motorways weren't as good as they are today. Travelling from one country to the next and going through all those border controls took ages, so driving all the way to Bratislava for just one show seemed silly. It was decided, therefore, that we should stop off in Holland on the way down to make the most of the trip; and as we were all relatively new to driving on the Continent, we agreed to travel in tandem, just in case we strayed off the beaten track. Talk about 'Five Go Mad in Dorset', this was more like 'Four Get Lost in Europe'...

So Andy and I teamed up in one lorry, with James and Paul in the other. First stop was to be Geesteren in Holland. I took some comfort in the knowledge that Andy, who was driving that leg of the journey, had lived in Holland for a number of years, so he obviously knew the country, or at least we hoped he did. I trusted that he knew where he was going so I was more than a bit relieved that I wouldn't have to endure the responsibility of map reading. There's always much grief to be piled onto the poor sod who sends you off in the wrong direction. But the journey passed without incident, although I do remember thinking it was taking a bloody long time to get there, as it hadn't looked that far on the map. And then we finally arrived at our destination – but no horse show. We couldn't understand where we'd gone wrong, Geesteren had been signposted and it all seemed like plain sailing. Then Andy realised: there are two Geesterens in Holland and, of course, he'd brought us to the wrong one. We were literally four hours in the wrong direction.

The prospect of turning round and driving back for another four hours was a complete drain on our spirits and had we known what we do now, we might have decided to stay put. After finally arriving, we had a dreadful show – not one of us jumped clear. How could we possibly go on to Bratislava to represent our country in a Nations Cup when we were all so hopeless? I subsequently discovered, however, that Geesteren is renowned as one of the toughest shows in Europe, and beating myself up about it was pretty pointless – and demoralising. Competing at Geesteren was tantamount to getting a good hiding before you went into a fight. In hindsight, we should have gone to an easier show to give us a bit of confidence, but we were all naive, wet behind the ears and hadn't thought it through properly. We needed something to lift our spirits.

I'm not sure that a drive through Munich on the way to Bratislava was going to do that, but it was just about the only option open to us and to cap it all, was going to take us about a day. Still, it was a lovely day and if anything was going to get us off to a bright and breezy start, it was the weather. It was particularly warm – in fact, unbelievably hot – so we got out on the road first thing and soon forgot our troubles as we trucked along. Now, in those days, there weren't limiters on the lorries to check our speed and some of these big trucks can really shift, making light of their load as they thunder along at 70 or 75mph. On the Continent, however, they're a lot stricter about the speed limits and we'd hardly gone any distance – about an hour-and-a-half – before we were pulled over for breaking the speed limit.

After a disastrous weekend showjumping in Geesteren, this was not what we needed and could seriously have added to our woes had it not been for the generous cop who took pity on us with just a warning, much to everyone's relief. To be fair, though, Andy's 18-ton Renault was a pretty good wagon in its day and although it wasn't very powerful, its high-speed back axle made it very quick – and consequently good on the flat in Holland. In Germany and Switzerland, however, as soon as it saw a hill, it would nap like hell. James and Paul's Volvo, however, wasn't quite as fast as ours on the flat, but surpassed it on the hills because it had a bit more torque.

So there followed a game of tag for the next 10 hours whereby on every flat stretch of road, Andy and I would sail past James and Paul with ease, only to have the smug look wiped off our faces as soon as we came to a hill. No matter how much encouragement we gave our poor lorry as it struggled with the slightest incline, it couldn't compete with the power of the Volvo. After a couple of hours, however, the novelty of these wacky races started to wear off and we were all beginning to go stir crazy, desperately trying to think of new ways to amuse ourselves. The outside temperature was hot to say the least, but nothing compared to our stiflingly hot, stuffy cab. This was in the days before air-conditioning and the heat was unbearable, so we rolled along with no shirts on and with the windows wide open, our arms getting truckers' tans as we rested them on the open window, the welcome breeze offering some attempt to cool us down.

We were all getting uncomfortable in the heat and our brains were beginning to frazzle with the sheer monotony of motorway driving – in fact, we probably could all have died of boredom had it not been for a used, dried teabag that suddenly came winging its way into our cab as Paul and James overtook us yet again – obviously their attempt at injecting a bit of fun into what had been a humourless 12 hours since we'd flopped in the showjumping arena. I'd been quick to dodge it, but it caught Andy smack on the cheek as he drove along, bursting and showering him in tiny tea leaves that covered his sweaty face in child-like little freckles. It was hilarious! I clutched my sides and roared with laughter while Andy stared ahead stone-faced. This was war – they'd thrown down the gauntlet. It was time to get even and return the compliment. We were like a bunch of kids, probably because we were only kids, but all these shenanigans helped us pass the time and gave us all a good laugh.

So here we all were the four of us on our way to Bratislava, playing silly beggars and the fun was just beginning. I remember scrambling from the cab into the living area in the back of the lorry to look for missiles with a good trajectory that would stun Paul and James as they came alongside. So I grabbed the nearest bucket and filled it with water – perfect ammo! The window in the living area was wide open – it was the perfect vantage point for launching an unexpected attack. All we had to do was wait for them to creep alongside us.

I popped my head gingerly out of the window – they were gaining on us, our lorry groaning in objection as Andy dropped down a gear to tackle the hill ahead. This was a steep hill, so I was going to have a bit of time to get my aim just right and time the attack perfectly. The Volvo inched its way towards us and then as soon as they were alongside us, I let loose with the water and caught them fair and square, taking them completely by surprise. Whoosh! The water slapped against the side of their lorry, but most of it caught poor James full on. He resembled the proverbial drowned rat! Gotcha! He did well not to swerve and crash but that possibility hadn't even crossed my mind.

This went on for a while and we all ached from laughing so much, all soaked to the skin as no one escaped a tit-for-tat dowsing. It was time to stop for a breather and swap drivers – it was my turn at the wheel now. We set off with the silliest grins on our faces, passing and re-passing each other depending on the terrain. Whoever said a 10-hour journey couldn't be fun?

"Next time they pass us, I'm going to moon at them," announced Andy out of the blue, which seemed like a great idea at the time. So we watched and waited for the next hill to appear on the horizon and sure enough, there it was, this little bump rising out of the tarmac. At the start of the incline, it was Andy's big moment and amid demented cackling, he started to undo his belt. Andy had the biggest, cheesiest, stupidest grin on his face as Paul and James started to pull alongside us, then with me giving him the signal, he proceeded to drop his trousers and stick his backside out the window – making it more of an eclipse than a moon.

By this point, I was practically crying with laughter, the tears rolling uncontrollably down my cheeks, as I tried to imagine what on earth this must have looked like from the other lorry – and to other drivers. Andy, too, was doubled up laughing, his body contorted and shaking as he gasped for breath. I can still hear his mad, demented laugh and picture his face scrunched up, almost in pain, through laughing so much.

But then his facial expression changed – the eyes went wide and saucer-like and there followed a deafening scream that would have woken the dead. As the scream rang out, piercing and cutting as it sliced through the stuffy atmosphere of the cab, he shot across towards me, clutching his backside, nearly sending me flying from the driver's seat, shouting that James and Paul had shot at him with an air rifle.

Now imagine if you will a German bumble bee, whose sole task was to try and cross the autobahn that afternoon, when out of the blue from nowhere an Englishman's hairy rear end hits you doing 70mph. The only line of defence for Herr Bee was to sting his attacker and Andy got it right on his freckle!

Cream was duly applied to Andy's backside and he spent the rest of the journey shuffling around, feeling sorry for himself and trying to get comfortable. He travelled the rest of the journey in agonised silence until we reached Munich where we stopped for the night and had a few bevvies – in Andy's case to numb the pain and take his mind off a sore bum which, he informed me, was swelling uncontrollably. Strange, but none of us felt the urge to inspect the damage – we were happy to take his word for it. We did try to muster a few words of sympathy in between bouts of stifled laughter, advising him to sleep on his front.

Next morning, Andy's pain in the butt had subsided dramatically, which was just as well, because we still had a fair way to go until we reached Bratislava. The city still had quite an 'Iron Curtain' feel to it and it took us an age to get through the border, Czechoslovakia being still very much under military control. Mind you, I think a lot depended on whether the border guards liked the look of you and that day, they obviously didn't take to us, because it took six hours to get through. Admittedly, I'm not the greatest traveller in the world, being easily irritated by delays and all the faffing around that goes on at airports, but this was something else. There was a lot of unnecessary shouting, a lot of hustle and bustle and to top it all, we had guns pointed at us for no apparent reason. I found it very unnerving.

Chapter 11

Boys' night out

- Building stables in Bratislava
- Performing the Fosbury Flop
- My bucking bronco
- My first international Grand Prix win

It was getting late when we finally reached the showground in Bratislava. We'd been on the road for about 16 hours that day, so were relieved that we could now unload the horses and get them settled for the night. What's more, we were the first to arrive, so that meant being able to get our pick of the stables – except there weren't any. All there was was a large, indoor school-type barn with a rope stretched across from one side to the other, to which we were expected to tie our horses – and that was the stabling for all the competition horses. No partitions, no bedding, no nothing.

So, unbelievable though it was and always one for trying to make the best of a bad situation, I suggested we build our own stabling. And of course, coming from a family of builders, where construction was in the blood, meant that I had a head start. In Bratislava, however, we had nothing in the way of power tools to help us build a row of four stables for our horses and the most we could rustle up in the way of materials when we went scavenging around the yard were some wooden pallets. So we set about with a hammer and a few bits of rope knocking up some makeshift stables, complete with rickety doors and dividing walls made out of sheets and towels. Ingenious! We were so proud of our efforts that we decided to celebrate in the bar where the local drink was something called Borovicka, a sort of schnapps-type spirit and the Slovak national drink – made from juniper berries I've since been told and good for the metabolism. We probably weren't too worried about its constitutional benefits then, more about whether it could hit the spot, as we'd had a long day on the road and now needed to relax and mull over the day's events.

We had a couple of lagers to loosen up, then decided to give the local brew a try – when in Rome and all that. We got stuck into shots of the stuff like it was going out of fashion and it soon became apparent that we were all pretty drunk. Then one bright spark, for whatever reason, decided that it would be a great idea to have a high-jumping competition before the show started. Why high-jump specifically I've no idea, but probably because there was an inviting privet hedge outside the bar and it seemed a shame not to make use of it. The idea was to see who could clear it with the most grace and athleticism, demonstrating that unique high-jump technique, the Fosbury Flop, a style employed by most high-jumpers as they jump back-first over the bar.

It wasn't an easy feat considering we were all completely smashed, but there was one important aspect of our daring little game that we'd overlooked – the landing site was pure gravel. You can imagine what it felt like crashing down on that, our boozy bodies totally oblivious to any pain, the gravel ripping holes in our clothes. We were all in a complete state, our clothes ruined by our antics and blood pouring out of pit marks on the exposed skin where the gravel had become embedded.

How we managed to stagger back to our lorries, I'll never know and none of us made it into bed that night – that would have involved too much exertion and co-ordination to take off our clothes. James Fisher did manage to stumble up into the front cab, while Andy Austin and Paul Sutton both took refuge on the floor in the back of the lorry. I ended up sleeping underneath the lorry. I woke up early next morning at about 5am and

I was wet with early-morning dew, but my back was stinging, almost as if the skin had been peeled off, and my initial reaction was that I'd be lying in something that was burning, like petrol or diesel. Skin had been stripped from my back and blood was seeping through my shirt – I was in a hell of a state. What a great way to tackle my first-ever Nations Cup, on the day before my birthday. But I only had myself to blame.

Clearly, we weren't in any fit state that morning even to fix ourselves a cup of coffee, let alone go around a showjumping course representing our country. It was just lucky that we had a day to recover. We were all like zombies. My churning stomach and red-raw back were painful reminders of our silly antics the night before. We were so poorly that we decided to check into our hotel a day early to pull ourselves together and get a decent night's sleep before the competition.

All told, going to Bratislava was a real eye opener for me, because I'd never been to a Communist bloc country before. Bratislava itself was not exactly warm and welcoming. The town seemed soul-less, a concrete jungle with buildings made of grey breeze blocks, stacked high like a child's Lego tower. The shops, too, were sparse with stocks running only to toothpaste, galvanised buckets and the odd bar of soap. There was hardly any fresh produce, like bread or luxuries like chocolate; and all the taxis and cars were Skodas, which in those days was a pretty crummy make.

Town centre aside, the Nations Cup went all right. We came second, with me jumping four and clear and I was placed in the Grand Prix, so overall we had a pretty good show in spite of the shaky start. However, as well as winning some cut-glass, our winnings were paid in the local currency which couldn't be taken out of the country, so we filled the lorries up with diesel and bought crates of Coca-Cola to take back with us. It was an eventful trip all told and served as a good introduction to what life is like on the road as a British team member. Really, nothing much has changed in the last 20-odd years as far as camaraderie is concerned. Competing as individuals, we are all fiercely competitive; but put us together on a team and you have a different animal altogether.

If anyone had ever told me that my next showjumping superstar was going to be a bucking bronco from Australia, I'd have laughed in their face. But there he'd been, this little chestnut fella, tied up to the collecting ring fence when Australian showjumper, Jeff McVean, spotted him in his headlights as he drove away from an evening with friends in the local bar. Jeff, who was based in the UK and riding for a wealthy Australian tycoon called Laurie Connell, had been in Perth, Western Australia, visiting family and had seen this horse, called The Frog, jump at a local show. Then coincidentally, as he'd been driving away at the end of the evening, Jeff saw The Frog tied up to the collecting ring fence fully tacked up. He went back into the bar to tell them about the horse, thinking that someone had forgotten him or was having a bit of a joke.

"Oh no, mate, that was us," piped up a drunken voice from the corner of the room. "We're going to have a skinful here tonight, so we thought we'd get the horse ready for the first class in the morning so that we can just get up, get on and get going."

So Jeff, who had felt sorry for the poor horse, decided to buy him on the spot and ship him to the UK.

"When you first get on him," his owners, a couple of rough and ready lads, had told Jeff, "you've got to be careful, because we've used him as a bucking horse to make a bit of money."

They'd set up an impromptu arena in the village, attach a bucking strap and use him as a rodeo horse, charging local lads five dollars a go and paying out 100 bucks if they could stay on him. So when you first got on him, you'd have to sit very quietly, as he'd arch his back and if you put your leg on, chances are he'd have you off as soon as look at you. He was an expert at dumping you and I fell off him loads of times.

But The Frog was a talented little horse and he was number five in Jeff's string, but was to be number one in mine and I went on to compete at some really big shows with him. While he wasn't a big horse, at just 15.3hh, he was one of the bravest, toughest horses I've ever sat on, even to this day – he had a massive heart, was really genuine and as tough as old boots. He was a real trier, however, like a springy rubber ball, who gave 100% all the time.

Jeff flew The Frog back to the UK and started jumping him straightaway in a few bigger classes, competing at Olympia and in a couple of internationals. He had a lot of success with the horse who, luckily for me, came on the market just at the right time. We decided we needed an injection of horsepower to my string of horses at the Meyerdings', so it was with this in mind that I went to try him and fell in love with him. Susan and Lutz decided to buy him for me.

Although I was holding my own on the national circuit, The Frog was just what I needed to be more competitive on the international scene with the likes of John and Michael Whitaker, Nick Skelton, Malcolm Pyrah, Geoff Billington, Joe Turi and Robert Smith all around at the time. These guys were in a different league altogether, so there was definitely some catching up to do on my part. If they were Premier Division, I was First Division and while they were usually picked for Nations Cups in prestigious venues such as Dublin, Calgary, Rotterdam and Aachen, I'd be at less important internationals and other Nations Cups. However, credit where credit's due, I was now qualifying on a regular basis for Horse of the Year Show, the Royal International and Olympia.

The dynamic on the yard at the Meyerdings' was also changing. Having been originally employed as Susan and Lutz's groom/rider, I was now doing more riding than anything else. People were sending their horses to me to ride and I was beginning to accumulate a nice string. But the special one at the time was undoubtedly The Frog. It was fitting then that he joined Supermarket on a trip to France, in Lorient.

It was a beautiful showground and everyone was very friendly and relaxed. I was riding Supermarket in the puissance and The Frog in the Grand Prix. I remember feeling great before the Grand Prix that day and justifiably so, because I'd ended up winning the puissance with Supermarket, who made the class look like a walk in the park. He flew around the course, making light of the fences and popping the 7ft wall with ease. Understandably, I felt confident and thought that there was literally nothing I couldn't do now, an attitude that turned round to bite me in the bum before I knew what had hit me. So now it was the turn of The Frog.

There had been a terrific thunderstorm in the afternoon and everywhere was wet and muddy, which left the collecting ring like a swamp, but the main arena wasn't as waterlogged and the going obviously suited The Frog because we jumped clear in the first round. My confidence was riding high and I remember thinking that I was so close to winning my first international Grand Prix. I tried to imagine what it would feel like cantering around the arena, riding hat in hand, waving to the cheering crowds… Dangerous thoughts, it's wrong to count your chickens and something I never do these days. As we all know, it can go spectacularly wrong as easily as it can go spectacularly right.

One thing was for sure, though, I was in it to win it. My little horse felt good underneath me. It would have been so easy to forego my ritual warm-up because he felt so highly tuned. But that would have been foolish, so I took him through his warm-up, jumping my routine big oxer towards the end. The Frog felt great, but as I came into the fence, I thought I'd wait for a deeper stride just to test him a bit – he felt up for it. For whatever reason, though, he picked up a complete stride too early, took off, paddled the jump, got the back rail caught between his front legs and tipped up.

As he landed, he hit the mud and then slid for about 10 yards. Not surprisingly, we parted company, but he was quick to pick himself up then gallop flat-out 500 yards across the park, back to where the lorries were parked on the hard-standing. I watched him go, terrified in case he fell. But he managed to stay upright and almost paused for a split second as if looking for his lorry, then recognising it, shot straight up the ramp and into his partition, where he stood shaking like a leaf waiting for someone to get him. When I reached him, I couldn't believe my eyes. The whole of one side was covered in thick, wet mud, this pretty little chestnut horse looking like something that had been dragged in from the swamp. And I looked as if I'd gone six rounds in a mud-wrestling contest, because I was also covered in mud from top to toe. One side of each of us was covered in muck; the other, immaculate. We both looked a sight. Not to be deterred by our appearance, however, there was work to be done, so I jumped on-board, cantered once around the collecting ring and jumped one vertical just as they were calling for me to go into the ring.

It was a beautiful round, mud or no mud, and I won it – my first-ever international Grand Prix. I was ecstatic; and when I looked down at my quirky little 15.3hh horse, I felt so proud of him, this little Australian bucking bronco who was now a Grand Prix winner. He'd come a long way in such a short space of time and as the National Anthem played, I didn't know whether to laugh or cry – cry because I was happy with the emotion of it all or laugh because we were both covered in wet, claggy mud.

To say I was chuffed with The Frog is an understatement, he was worth his weight in gold and I was really happy for the Meyerdings. From there, he went on to win lots of classes, jumping some of the biggest tracks in World Cup competitions and coming fourth in the King George V Gold Cup, so I was already hot on the trail of Mike Saywell to win the trophy I'd seen him scoop on the telly that night when I was 12. My heart was still set firmly on emulating my hero's success.

The Frog was a fantastic horse and he suited me down to the ground because I liked the fact that he was brave and tenacious. What's more, I had total belief in him, although it was soon to be eclipsed by, of all things, a Thoroughbred racehorse.

Chapter 12

A changing dynamic

- My showjumping steeplechaser
- Going it alone
- Exhilarating times
- Losing The Frog

While ex-racehorses seem to find their way into eventing these days, there aren't many in showjumping. That's probably because we have a 'single discipline' as opposed to a 'multi-discipline' mentality, with horses being bred specifically for our chosen regime. I am, however, all for giving horses who haven't been successful in one discipline a chance to try their hand at another and I don't think there's as much of a cross-over as there should be. What's more, if anyone brings me a horse who's failed in one discipline, I'll try not to be judgemental about its potential based on its breeding. I want to judge a horse on his own merits, not because his sire was a prolific showjumping or dressage stallion.

When I consider what makes a top horse, it's not always down to the breeding. For me, the horse has to be careful and brave. But then if he's too brave, he's probably not that careful, and if he's too careful, chances are he's not that brave so it's a vicious circle. And when you consider attitude – or strength of character – a lot of the top horses are a bit quirky.

I stumbled across Mighty McGuigan (James) the following

year when I returned to Lorient. He was ridden by showjumper Mike Florence and owned by Eugene and Catherine O'Neill. But there were issues surrounding the horse's behaviour as a racehorse – he used to get anxious about having other horses boxing him in on the rails. He'd lash out at them and on one occasion, he made contact with a jockey and broke his leg.

In order to get the horse used to company, James's trainer David Nicholls – The Duke – had suggested he was taken showjumping in the winter, to mix with other horses in the collecting ring. So racing enthusiasts Eugene and Catherine, who were not familiar with the showjumping scene, had asked Mike Florence to socialise him ready for the following season's race calendar. But they hadn't been prepared for this horse's incredible talent over fences that saw him go from novice to Grade A in about nine months. He was astonishing and did nothing but win classes left, right and centre. In fact, such was his success as a showjumper that he didn't go back to racing. He performed out of sheer instinct and natural talent, not from a build-up of gradual, specific training, the likes of which I undertake with youngsters or newcomers to showjumping.

At Lorient, I spent some time watching Mike jumping James and realised what a special horse he was. I enquired to see if he might be for sale but he was going well for Mike with a few notable wins under his belt and wasn't available. All that was about to change, however. When I saw them again at the Three Counties Show, horse and rider weren't quite the picture they'd been in Lorient, as James had started to stop at combinations. He'd begun to suffer with tunnel vision and panic. If he hit a fence, he'd panic even more which led to him quickening through his combinations and getting the distance wrong, so he'd hit the jumps and fret even more.

It was at that point that I received a call from Catherine and Eugene asking if I'd like to take James on. Mike thought the horse had lost his bottle. The horse was typically 'upside down' in his way of going, in that he went at speed with his head held high and his back hollow, as is common with racehorses. James hadn't had much basic schooling so he hadn't learnt how to work correctly or to shorten his canter stride when he was asked and his jump tended to get flat and fast.

As James started to jump bigger courses, it became harder for him to adjust his stride to the distance between fences in combinations, so he'd panic and rush. What he was lacking was basic training, technique, a solid foundation. In short, he'd had a meteoric rise to fame and when the wheels fell off, he had no experience or training to fall back on to get him out of trouble.

James obviously loved jumping and it was a real shame to see him getting into such a tangle with it, to have such a mental block about it. But I had no intention of giving up on him, I just needed to work on a few basic principles. In James's case, whenever he saw a combination of three fences in a row at a competition, he'd panic and stop. So the horse – who was eight at the time – came to the Meyerdings' yard for six months. I made a decision not to enter any competitions that contained combinations or even doubles and then I'd do completely the opposite at home, jumping nothing but doubles and combinations.

At shows, the poor horse had got his knickers in such a twist worrying about combinations that he'd started looking for them, so I'd just compete him in Top Score and speed classes, where there'd either be no combinations or I had the option of missing them out altogether. Then at home, I'd jump him down grid after grid so that he'd get used to seeing four or five fences in a row, but on home ground in his own comfortable environment. That did the trick, because at the Three Counties Show six months later, I won the Open which involved us jumping a combination.

I was thrilled as it would have been a huge waste of a terrific horse if I'd failed, but I'd gone into the project feeling confident, trying to understand what makes some horses tick and others throw in the towel. What's more, I enjoyed the challenge and found it rewarding when I got to the bottom of a problem and came out the other side successfully. And thank God James did, because he was the most careful, scopey blood horse I've ever ridden. Not only that, he was incredibly quick and one of life's enthusiasts. He had amazing energy, loved his jumping and was such a natural technician that you could hear his front feet slap hard on his belly as he picked up in front over a jump. When he was on song, he was an unbelievable jumping machine.

More and more owners were sending me their horses to ride – in fact, in 1991, there were a dozen or so horses on the yard, but only one belonged to Susan and Lutz. Although I was still technically their groom/rider and still earning £70 a week, I was beginning to get itchy feet and considered whether I should be starting my own business. After all, I'd got the clientele, so this was surely the next step for me.

I went to see John Cosgrove and asked his advice on how to make the next move – without his support, I probably wouldn't have had the courage to make the approach to Susan and Lutz. Admittedly, I wasn't sure how the Meyerdings would take the news that I wanted to reconsider my position on the yard and start my own business. They were fantastic employers and I'd been with them a long time, but I was nervous of their reaction. They could, however, see that things had changed and agreed that my proposal to rent the yard from them made perfect sense. So I took it on for £400 a week, with my focus now on riding and competing all the horses myself. It was the perfect arrangement for both parties – after all, the Meyerdings had been good to me and supported me, so not upsetting them was a priority.

One of the things I needed to organise first was getting my own lorry, as I was keen to establish some form of independence. I'd managed to save £13,000 while working for Susan and Lutz and heard that the late Caroline Bradley's old wagon, a Ford D series, was up for sale – it was on the market for £8,000, could hold seven horses and had a good living area. The lorry was in a seriously bad way, as I don't think it had been used regularly since her tragic death nearly a decade before. It hadn't even been driven for more than a year when I went to see it and weeds were growing up through the engine.

Tony Wade, my very good friend who's sadly no longer with us, came with me to collect it from Norfolk. We managed to get the vehicle started – eventually – but as soon as we began moving it, vital bits would fall off and we discovered a bird's nest between one of the partitions and the wall. Once we'd patched everything back into place, we got the lorry home and into a friend's barn, where we'd spend hours rubbing down, T-cutting and getting it back into shape. When we'd finished, it looked like a million dollars.

Being involved in its restoration like this took me back to the time when Dad bought the railway wagon and converted it into a horsebox for me – it felt like history repeating itself. Having my own lorry now meant I didn't have to rely on Susan's. It also meant I'd now have to be responsible for entering my own shows. Up until then, that had all been taken care of for me by Susan and Lutz and I'd just have to be ready and turn up at the show.

Of course, the housekeeping includes necessities of the job – the entry forms, keeping tabs on which horse is placed in which competition, maintaining veterinary histories of each horse, organising training sessions and lessons, planning lecture-demos into a schedule that is always running at full capacity, keeping on top of social media like Facebook and Twitter. There's also a lot of pulling together involved at home to make the business a success – it's not just about what happens in the ring. Team Stockdale is like a well-oiled machine that needs constant refuelling to keep it on the road.

While winning is important to me, what is equally gratifying is producing consistent, top-level horses from youngsters, something I know I'm reasonably good at. It's not just about winning the red rosettes, although that did bring with it a certain amount of recognition. There was, however, the constant reminder that the David Broomes of this world, the Graham Fletchers, were still on that next level up and I wanted to be up there with them. While I felt comfortable around them, I wasn't comfortable sitting at the same table with them. That changed, however, when I won the puissance at Horse of the Year Show on Supermarket in 1991 – a real turning point.

It came down to the final round with just Michael Whitaker on Didi and me on Supermarket. Both of us faulted so it was judged we would be joint first. However, both Michael and I said we'd like to have another go and the judges agreed. It was announced to the departing audience, who all rushed back to their seats, heightening the tension. We both jumped again and cleared the wall with the crowd going crazy and Raymond Brooks-Ward screaming with excitement over the PA. So in the end, we split the prize money. It made great viewing and the next morning was on 'Breakfast TV'.

This period was probably one of the most exhilarating times of my career, when I went from employee to employer. But with that exhilaration came a harsh lesson about the 'business' of showjumping when I sold a pony within four days of starting my business. I made about £200 profit and they paid me in cash, in £20 notes, all of which were counterfeit, something I discovered when I went to buy a celebratory Chinese meal that night. I kept just one £20 note in a frame at home as a salutary reminder.

Little did I know that another bombshell was just around the corner. I was loading up the lorry to go to a show at Vicarage Farm when Lutz told me to take The Frog off the lorry – Malcolm Pyrah apparently had a customer coming from America to buy him. He was to go to Malcolm to be trained for this customer. I thought this strange and suggested that I would train him. But Lutz was insistent that The Frog was leaving the yard and would hear nothing of my offers to at least deliver him to Malcolm. I was devastated. I'd grown attached to this little horse and couldn't understand what was happening. Was Lutz taking him away from me because I'd done something wrong? Was he now letting Malcolm have the ride for some reason? I had no idea and still don't know to this day why The Frog left so quickly.

I went to Vicarage Farm that day, upset, distraught and feeling that the rug had been pulled from under my feet and when I returned home later that day, I'd secretly hoped that the deal had fallen through, that The Frog would be standing in his stable. No such luck – his stable was empty and he'd gone. I don't know what happened to the customer but Malcolm had him for about a year, jumping him at Olympia and some of the bigger shows. It had been a real wrench for me.

I'm not a bitter person, but I couldn't help but feel a slight satisfaction in knowing that the horse didn't go as well for Malcolm as he had done for me. I'm sure that The Frog could have gone on to even bigger and better things, but we hadn't been given the chance to prove our partnership. So the euphoria at setting up on my own was short-lived, with two devastating blows to the business that came from nowhere.

Chapter 13

Who's that girl?

- Laura Cocklin
- A yard of my own
- Two is better than one
- The perfect present

Although I was still smarting from losing my best horse just three weeks after setting up my own business at the Meyerdings', there just wasn't enough time in the day to bear grudges. I was still busy with my other horses, namely Supermarket, who I was using more for the puissance classes; Mighty McGuigan, who was fast becoming top of my string; and a newcomer called Sarlydun Lad, who'd been with John Whitaker. The owner, John Duncan, lived locally in Barnet and asked if I would consider taking him on, seeing that John Whitaker lived such a distance away in Yorkshire. He didn't have to ask twice.

The County Show circuit was a great hunting ground for a young showjumper like me, cutting my teeth in an industry that was competitive to the extreme. But it was a run of shows in September 1991, starting with Henley, which provided the richest pickings for me in more ways than one. It was to change my life forever. This was where I first spotted Laura Cocklin, a pretty, smiling, blonde girl who was grooming for Ernest Dillon at the show. I thought she was lovely – so much so that I couldn't take my eyes off her all day. I noticed that she seemed to be with a lad and it transpired that he was Ernest Dillon's son, Tom, and that she was going out with him. But I also noticed when she looked at me – it wasn't just a fleeting glance, more a meaningful stare. I was sure the cheeky lass was giving me the eye.

I didn't talk to Laura that day because I couldn't pluck up the courage, but I saw her the following week at the Camberley Show, again helping Ernest, so I thought I had better pull myself together. Now this may come as a surprise that I am quite shy, but this girl had knocked me for six.

"I don't know who that girl is helping you," I said to Ernest as casually as I could, "but I was, err, wondering if you might introduce us?"

I couldn't quite believe I was going through with this. I was essentially asking this man to introduce me to his son's girlfriend. Ernest didn't turn a hair – he called her over, introduced us, then made some lame excuse about having to go to sort his draw-reins out. Talk about obvious. What he thought about me wanting to chat up his son's girlfriend remains a mystery. So Laura and I had a chat and, after my initial panic, I felt totally at ease with her. She was very warm and open, with the most beautiful smile I think I'd ever seen. She was friendly and I got the distinct impression that she was as interested in me as I was in her. I was smitten and left with the feeling that I definitely wanted to see more of Laura.

Over the next few days, I couldn't get Laura out of my mind and hoped that she might be at the Newbury Show the following week. Thank goodness she was, because I'd already made up my mind that I was going to ask her out. I'd been rehearsing over and over again what I was going to say to her, and didn't think for one second that she might turn me down. I had a good feeling about this and luckily I was rewarded with a 'yes'. If she'd have said 'no', I don't know what I would have done.

Our first date involved me driving down to West Sussex where she was living, as I'd planned to go and have a look at some horses – or at least that's what I told her. I didn't want her to gain the impression that I was making a special journey – which of course I was. I wanted to play it cool and casual. Anyway, the ruse was that I was going to try a horse at Ernest Dillon's yard, so did she want to come for a drink afterwards? While the exact details of our first date remain a bit hazy, one thing I do remember is that driving home that night, I knew that this was something special. We started seeing each other regularly after that and things started to snowball pretty quickly. We enjoyed each other's company and, of course, because horses were such a big part of our lives, we were never lost for anything to talk about. She understood the rollercoaster nature of the industry – the highs, the lows, the successes, the disappointments and the falls, and of course, she has seen me through a few of those in her time, not least when I broke my collarbone (one of many broken over the years) a couple of weeks after we met.

A pupil's horse had fallen at a fence when I was teaching them and the horse had slammed into the deck, all just a few days before a dinner date with Laura and then Horse of the Year Show. But we still made plans to go out to the China Diner, a posh Chinese restaurant in Beaconsfield. I was wearing a clavical brace which was a bit like a bra and designed to hold everything in place, but it really restricted my movement and it was pretty uncomfortable, so cutting up food was near impossible. I was totally incapacitated a) because of the pain I was in and b) because of the contraption I was wearing. I had tried to remain stoic and unaffected for the first part of the date but Laura, sensing my frustration and helplessness, started to cut up all my food so that I could spear it with a fork. I remember thinking at the time that I'd found a good 'un, a real caring soul.

While some of the details and dates surrounding our courtship remain a bit fuzzy, I can remember clearly what Laura was wearing that evening when she came to Horse of the Year Show – a blue Chanel-type suit – because she looked fabulous, absolutely stunning. I walked around the corner to meet her and thought, 'Wow'! Talk about making an impression. But I like to think I impressed her equally that night when I came second in the puissance on Supermarket – with a broken collarbone – a fact that hadn't gone unnoticed by my mates at the show.

"If she doesn't think you're hot property after that perform-ance, then you'd better think of another way of impressing her!" Steven Smith roared with laughter.

It was all change for me. As well as having a new girlfriend, the end of 1991 saw my life take on another new dimension. I soon realised I was outgrowing the Meyerdings' yard. I was now being sent more horses to ride by various owners. I had no alter-native but to up sticks and upsize to larger premises. I'd already given Susan and Lutz notice to quit, so once the dust had settled after Horse of the Year Show, I sought larger premises. I'd heard of an old dairy that was available to rent in Chesham, Buckinghamshire, about four miles as the crow flies from Susan and Lutz's yard.

Moving out of the Meyerdings' was exciting and daunting all at the same time, as now I really was on my own – no Lutz or Susan to fall back on in times of a crisis. And no cosy, comfort-able staff cottage to call my own. Instead, I spent the first six months living in my lorry. I created my own little home from home, complete with mod cons. I ran an extension lead through one of the louvre windows in the lorry so I could at least watch TV and have a heater on, and I also managed to rig up a phone line. I had a small living area with an oven and a shower situated in one of the partitions, but no loo. But this was all right for me, it was perfect, especially as this was the lorry I'd lovingly restored. My lorry was my pride and joy and I was as happy as Larry – although unhitching it all so I could go to a show was a complete pain in the butt.

The whole set-up, understandably, was not exactly ideal for Laura who was at this stage coming up to see me at weekends on a regular basis. The bathroom facilities were not up to scratch in her opinion and I must say I was surprised. In the corner of one of the empty stables, I'd rigged up what I thought was a perfectly adequate toilet – two big 45-gallon drums acting as a screen, behind which was a portable loo, the type you might take with you on a camping holiday. But while Laura seemed pretty impressed with my other makeshift mod cons, she drew the line at the loo and would refuse to use it, preferring to drive down to the local McDonald's instead.

Those were happy days for me, really really happy days, although bloody cold in the winter – invariably I'd wake with a little stream of frozen dribble on my pillow and I always made a point of getting dressed in my riding clothes the night before the following day. But everything was organised, with Laura religiously coming up to see me every weekend when she'd finished work on a Friday. At the time, she was living with her mum, Ann, and stepdad, Andrew Judge. She'd help exercise the horses with me and would groom for me at shows, although I had a couple of other staff working for me at that point, so the business was beginning to expand.

I obviously needed extra accommodation for my workers, so I bought a lovely mobile home for them, shipping it onto the premises under cover of darkness. It was like a military operation, but necessary due to strict planning regulations at the time, so I enlisted the help of half a dozen strong lads to help me roll it into position and push it 50 yards behind the farm buildings. Then just to make damn sure it wasn't going to be spotted by visiting dignitaries from the local council, we fenced it in and within 20 minutes of it hitting the floor, a big larch lap fence had gone up – I was taking no chances.

When I look back, that mobile home was a lot more palatial than my lorry and I could have done with it for Laura and me when she decided to move in with me permanently in 1992. There was no house on site, but plenty of spacious storage lofts above the barns and stables, all crying out for a refurbishment. All it took was one conversation with John Cosgrove and he was on the case, sending in a bunch of guys to convert one of the lofts into a cosy, livable space. Since those days when I used to teach him and his kids on a Tuesday evening at the Meyerdings' he has become a huge supporter of me and Laura, a pivotal part of our family, and here he was in those early days helping out wherever he could.

Our flat wasn't huge, but it was home, with a bedroom, kitchen area, bathroom and sitting room that my brother, Ivan, carpeted with an offcut that cost me a tenner – a fiver for the carpet and a fiver to him for helping. Laura and I were really happy there and for the first time in a long while, I was starting to feel comfortable with my lot. Everything in my life was beginning to fall into place.

Laura pitched up one Friday evening in her little yellow Jeep (great for using to harrow the arena), carrying a little cardboard box, which she handed over to me with a twinkle in her eye and a knowing smile on her lips. It was heavier than it looked and whatever was inside shuffled restlessly. I put it down on the mounting block, gingerly unfolding the cardboard lid in case this was Laura's idea of a joke and a Jack-in-the-box was going to leap out at me. Then I peered inside.

I would have loved to have been standing in Laura's shoes to see the reaction on my face. My heart just melted when I saw this tiny black and white fluffy bundle with its big brown, soulful eyes staring back at me – it was a Border collie pup, a tiny wee thing that we named Ben. She knew that I loved the breed, because my mum had one at the time. He became my shadow. He turned out to be a real character, a loyal companion who, when he wasn't following me around the yard, would sit at the bottom of the stairs of our converted loft guarding me and Laura as if his life depended on it. And then when we later moved to Dovecote Farm in Northamptonshire, where we live today, he'd do exactly the same – sit at the bottom of the stairs keeping watch over the family. He lived to a great old age – 18 – and is now buried in a little wooden box under a cherry tree near the house. He was a cracking dog.

Chapter 14

A baptism of fire

- Sponsorship – the way forward
- The showjumping Smurf
- Madrid Nations Cup – what a fandango!
- Down, but not out in Lisbon

1992 was turning into a very good year. Business was booming and the horses were going well. Then I got the call, the invitation to be part of the Nations Cup team in Madrid, which I had slight reservations about.

It was Olympic year and the Games were being held in Barcelona. Now, the word on the street was that Madrid was going to be the trials for the Spanish Olympic team and that it was going to be a tough, testing course. Obviously, most of the British big guns – Nick Skelton, Joe Turi, John and Michael Whitaker, Geoff Billington – were going to avoid it like the plague and not take their potential Olympic horses for fear of injury. So it was down to Muggins here on Mighty McGuigan; Warren Clarke riding Benjamin; Mark McCourt on La Paz; and Andy Austin on Orthos. The plan was to travel on to Madrid after Royal Windsor, although if the performance of Andy and Orthos was anything to go by, could we be wasting our time?

On the second day at Royal Windsor, Andy's round in the Gents' Championship started well and was an encouragement to the rest of the team, looking very promising until he came to the water jump. Although Orthos was a really talented horse, he clearly had a thing about water. Not only did he stop, but slam-dunked Andy straight into it head first, before galloping out of the ring with his bridle around his legs. Then out of the water jump emerged this vision of such blueness, we were convinced poor Andy had morphed into a Smurf. It was one of the funniest things I've ever seen in the ring and the more the rest of us tried not to laugh, the more difficult it was to keep a straight face. What astonished us was how blue he was, but then in those days the water trays were either painted with blue emulsion or they chucked in a 'Bloo Loo' toilet cleaner for added effect.

Seriously, though, apart from being concerned about travelling to Madrid with a Smurf, what good was a horse who was going to mess up at the water? What chance would we have in the Nations Cup? Understandably, tensions were now running high in the British camp – so much so that the BSJA selectors announced they were going to cancel the team to Madrid because Andy and his horse weren't fit to go and they didn't want to waste their money funding a non-competitive team. There was uproar, because we'd already invested a lot in the trip. Consequently, businessman Paul Stamp, who owned Orthos, offered to fund the trip if his horse let down the rest of the team in Madrid. It was a generous move and the selectors couldn't say fairer than that.

Sadly, it turned out to be one of the worst Nations Cup shows I've ever been to for all sorts of reasons – lack of camaraderie and team spirit, and the only horse who seemed to be jumping flawlessly was my own, Mighty McGuigan. Come the day, we knew we'd have no chance, especially if Orthos was going to have another paddy at the water. I felt a bit sorry for Malcolm Pyrah, who was the Chef d'Equipe and had a tough time holding the team together, because we were all falling out with one another. It was an uphill struggle.

On the day of the Nations Cup, Andy was first to go but again it was a shambles. He went clear up to the water, then 20 metres out from the fence, Orthos decided he wasn't going any further.

Andy turned him away and had another run at it. This time he got closer – in fact, right up to the edge of the jump – but Orthos still wouldn't attempt it. Andy had one last try – we were allowed three refusals before elimination in those days – and with a lot of pushing and shoving, and kicking and growling, he literally walked the horse through the water. At least Andy wasn't eliminated but he incurred 32 faults. We were glum. That was a cricket score. We now had no margin for error. Andy's was going to be the discarded score. So we all had to go clear or, at most, have four faults if we had any chance of pulling this back from the brink. We'd had a lucky escape and were lying second after the first round.

Come the second round, it was Andy in first again.

"Come on Andy, you can jump clear this time," an encouraging Malcolm told him as he rode down the tunnel to the arena. Andy didn't even acknowledge him or indeed any of us – whether he was ignoring the comment or didn't hear, I don't know. But judging from Andy's look of steely determination, I'd guess he was oblivious to what was going on around him. He was totally focused and I can't ever remember seeing another rider since with such determination. Once Andy had passed the rest of us, Malcolm quipped: "He'll never do it, he'll never go clear."

Andy, in fact, had a brilliant round but we could hardly bear to watch him as he approached the water. Orthos gave it the eye, half going to stop. But Andy was quick to react – he booted and smacked him with the whip, and he flew over it. Orthos had launched himself indignantly over and with that, Andy went clear. Then I went clear. In fact, we all went clear to win the Nations Cup. We were ecstatic. Against all the odds, we'd beaten every other nation around a really tough course – an Olympic trial course no less. Goodness knows how we did it, but I guess a lot of the praise has to go to Andy. I heard that after his disastrous first round, he hadn't got off Orthos – instead, he took him cantering through every puddle and bit of water he could find in the collecting ring and around the showground. He was determined that it wasn't going to be his horse who let the team down. 'Horse & Hound' called it the performance of the year.

We were so chuffed. How we did it, we still don't know to this day – and it's talked about a lot.

Fate, however, is fickle and from this high note, I came crashing down to earth with a bump. Andy and I had been invited to a brand-new show, set in beautiful gardens in the centre of Lisbon, run by Portuguese showjumper, Jorge Mateus, and his father. It had attracted good sponsorship and there was a decent amount of prize money up for grabs with 32 riders competing. But in-between Madrid and Lisbon, we decided to go home until the Thursday, having sent the horses on to Portugal by lorry. It gave me a few days to sort some things out at the yard and get the staff wages organised. Because the business was still in its infancy, money was tight and everything was done on a hand-to-mouth basis. But I was pretty good at keeping tabs on things, so I had no doubt there was enough money in my account to pay the staff.

I arrived at my bank, the TSB, wrote out a cheque for £400 cash – which is what I did every month – only to be told by the cashier that I didn't have enough funds in my account. I couldn't believe that I'd messed up my sums, but there was no persuading her. Furthermore, she told me to hand over my cheque book as I'd supposedly been writing cheques without sufficient funds to cover them. I was flabbergasted – how was I going to pay the girls? How was I going to buy feed for the horses, and groceries for me and Laura? I had to think on my feet, and fast. So I grabbed the cheque book from her, stuffed it into a pocket and legged it out of the bank, shouting behind me as I went:

"If you can catch me, you can have it!"

What on earth possessed me to do that? It was a totally instinctive, crazy reaction. I felt like a bank robber on the run, but as long as I had that cheque book, I still had something. What incensed me even more as I made my escape onto the high street was the offer in the TSB's window enticing students with a free £1,000 overdraft when they opened a new account – a free £1,000 overdraft and here I was, a customer with a business, an income and they wouldn't even give me 1p.

Fortunately, I remembered that Joe Turi owed me a bit of

money, about £200, from a show in Kiskunhalas, Hungary, so by the time I'd paid the girls their wages out of that, I had exactly £8 in my pocket to go to Lisbon with. I was, therefore, extremely relieved that we were picked up at the airport by the organisers of the show and equally grateful that they were putting us up in the five-star Hotel Tivoli, all expenses paid, because I had not a single penny to live off all week. The hotel was luxurious, slap bang in the middle of Lisbon, and they laid out all sorts of lovely presents in our rooms. Life doesn't get much better than this, I thought. And Laura was flying out to join me after work on Friday evening to stay until the Sunday. John Cosgrove came too to lend a bit of support, even though none of his horses were jumping there, but then that's John for you – thoughtful, considerate and selfless.

When I look back, I was living life on the edge. I was penniless and had no idea how I was going to afford to get the horses home after the show. In the grand scheme of things, I was completely broke – I had a business and a lorry, but no assets of my own, no house, I was renting a yard, I was skint. It was pitiful. So I pitched up at the show on the first day with nothing in my pocket, until Mighty McGuigan went out and won the first class and a £3,000 prize. What a horse, top man. I was triumphant and hopeful that I could, at least, get the horses home and have enough to buy some food. Overall, though, I was still in dire financial straits.

I decided that rather than jump James the next day, I'd rest him and save him for the Grand Prix – which, would you believe it, he also won. Only this time it was a whopping £21,000 to the winner. It was late-night jumping, about 12.30am, and I was presented with my prize with the National Anthem ringing out. 'My good God,' I thought, 'have I just dodged a bullet here or what?' James had been my saviour and dug me out of a very large hole.

With all these mixed emotions finally giving way to laughter, I went to do the accounts and collect my winnings, all £21,000 of it in cash. But they'd run out of larger denominational notes and only had the equivalent of £5 notes in Portuguese escudos.

By the time I'd paid the 20% tax, however, and deducted our entry fees, there was still over £18,000-worth of escudos which Laura packed into two plastic carrier bags and took back to the hotel along the streets of Lisbon at 2am, looking as if she'd just done the weekly shop at Sainsbury's. With all of us back at the hotel, John Cosgrove and I bought enough champagne to float a battleship – we stayed up all night drinking, not really believing what I'd achieved, and we toasted my escaping the breadline by the skin of my teeth.

Morning came and I was still too tipsy to care what I looked like, so I staggered onto the plane still in my riding gear. I looked a right state and had the mother of all hangovers, but it was worth it. My first job when we arrived back home was to go into the TSB in Chesham, where I ceremoniously deposited my two carrier bags of escudos at the foreign exchange desk and asked for them to be exchanged for the sterling equivalent. The look on the cashier's face was a picture – he obviously thought I'd robbed a bank – so I was called into the manager's office. He wanted to know where I'd got all the money from but obviously didn't believe me, because he rang the BSJA to verify the fact I'd won it in the Lisbon Grand Prix and that it wasn't stolen. After all, he didn't know who Tim Stockdale was or what I did. He just saw me as this funny little guy who wore stupid trousers for a living.

After I'd paid off all my debts and given James's owners, Catherine and Eugene O'Neill, their share of the winnings, there was about £8,000 left. So my next job was to withdraw every single penny of it and close my TSB account. Then I walked straight across the road and deposited the lot with NatWest – and they gave me a £1,000 overdraft. I've been with them ever since.

Following the success of Madrid and Lisbon, the British team selectors obviously thought I was a good bet for the Scandinavian tour, which was always a good trip. I was one of five – along with Philip Heffer, Mark McCourt, Matthew Lanni and Warren Clarke – to represent Great Britain at two Nations

Cups, at Falsterbo in Sweden and Drammen in Norway. It was while in Falsterbo that I was approached by Eurosport to do some commentating for them on the Swedish Derby. I wasn't competing in it, so thought it might be fun and good experience – another string to my bow. I also remembered something Dad said to me when I was a lad: "If you can speak about your sport, you'll always make money."

Dad's words struck a chord and I was determined to commentate my way, as if talking to a mate. I wanted my delivery to be viewer-friendly, relaxed and an honest representation of what was happening in the ring. Eurosport seemed to like that. So, if a rider had a nickname, I'd tell the viewers as much – as in Wazza for Warren Clarke. And if a rider made a mistake, I wasn't just going to say, 'Bad luck', I'd explain why the rider had crashed head-long into the fence or ended up in the drink.

I enjoyed my new-found venture thoroughly and was encouraged when the commentator I was sharing the bill with thought I was a seasoned trouper. It was a huge compliment and really boosted my confidence, as I'd never done anything like this before. It was new territory but I took to it like a duck to water and my parents were very proud hearing their son on telly. What I'm good at is talking about horses, but take me out of my comfort zone, and I'll go all shy and retiring. That day with Eurosport, however, formed a huge turning point in my life and created self-belief in my own ability. Since then, whenever radio and TV appearances have come along, I've jumped (sometimes, quite literally) at the chance.

The very next day, I was asked to do a programme in which I'd be filmed jumping over a Jaguar parked in the middle of a fence – the idea being to demonstrate how wide some of these fences can be. It was huge when they'd finished building it and I decided to use my second horse, Sarlydun Lad, but he kept bumping the front rail out – and he did this at least a dozen times. It was one of the most embarrassing things I've ever got involved in and something that was supposed to take two minutes to film, but ended up taking half-an-hour. The poor Jag had its wing mirror knocked off and was getting bumped and dented left, right and centre. Everyone on the film crew acted as if it was fine but every time the pole hit the car, I could hear the garage owners groaning.

I've often been asked what I would have done if Mighty McGuigan hadn't won in Lisbon: how I would have got the horses home? I tell them that I'd have gone to plan B, although there was never actually a plan B. But I would have raised the money somehow, probably by teaching. I did so much teaching at the Meyerdings', though – some days from 8am-10pm – that I almost came to resent it. Then, I would teach as many people as wanted a lesson but these days I just don't have the time. I'm therefore a bit selective and train only riders at the sharp end – those who are talented and serious about their showjumping.

So my clientele at Lye Green Farm was growing, as was the opportunity to go further afield to do lecture-demos and clinics for anyone who was keen enough to organise them – and I loved them. I'd teach all sorts of horses and riders, come across all sorts of issues. Because I had a good reputation for being able to fix just about any problem, it became a really satisfying part of my job, seeing improvements from week to week, month to month. It all felt so worthwhile and I got a huge kick out of watching talented horses and riders progress, and still do. However, it was while I was on one of my regular clinics in Jersey that I met another person who was about to make me an offer I couldn't refuse.

I'd received an invitation to a party that I knew would be rude to turn down. Everyone was really friendly and always made me feel welcome on Jersey, but I was pretty useless at walking into a room of complete strangers. I needn't have worried on this occasion, because these were lovely, genuine horsey people, so I felt completely at home. I was taken slightly aback, however, when this chap walked straight up to me, took my hand in a vice-like grip and announced very matter-of-factly: "My name is Philip Billington. I'm a course designer and BSJA Area Rep for Hampshire, and I'm going to sponsor you."

I wanted to grab Mr Philip Billington by the cheeks and plant a huge smacker on him there and then, but I thought better of it. Aware that I must have looked a proper Charlie, I managed to splutter out a 'thank you' before he handed me his business card, and told me to get my CV together and give him a call. Then he left. I was tongue-tied, excited, disbelieving – was this guy for real? I looked at the business card – he was Chairman and Chief Executive of a company called Chemring. They had just bought a clothing company called Toggi that specialised in cold-store clothing – overalls, jackets, gloves, hats, that sort of thing.

Sadly, Philip died from a heart attack in 2009 but not before he'd taken Toggi by the scruff of the neck and turned it into a successful equestrian brand. I remember my first official meeting with him as a potential member of Team Toggi. I went to see him in his swanky executive office near Southampton and put my CV on his desk. I'd spent hours getting it together with Laura's help because I haven't a clue how to work a computer. Everything was laid out clearly and concisely in chronological order and she'd put it into a neat little folder, so I was very proud of it, my first and only CV. I laid it on Philip's desk. He didn't even glance down.

"So, I'm going to sponsor you," he announced. "I'll give you £20,000 in the first year, £22,500 in the second and £25,000 in the third, then we'll reassess and see how things are working out. I want you to be as good as you can be and help where possible to promote the brand. How does that sound to you?"

"Perfect," I croaked, not really knowing what to say. "But aren't you going to look at my folder?" I whined, disappointed. I felt a complete fool, but it was the first thing that came into my head. Laura and I – well, Laura mainly – had lovingly created my CV and I thought the least he could do was go through it, discuss it and then negotiate. But knowing Philip as I do now, once he'd made up his mind to do something, that was it. He was going to do it. It wouldn't matter if he wasn't 100% right, as long as he was completely 100% convinced and committed to something, that's what counted. By the same token, if he didn't believe in something, there was no point trying to persuade him otherwise. There was no budging him, the man was not for turning.

Once Philip had managed to recruit a former Barbour Clothing executive to help set up the brand, Team Toggi was created with just two riders – me and eventer Blyth Tait. Later, course builder, Kelvin Bywater, came on-board. These were really happy days for me and I cherished my association with the company, because it was my first proper sponsorship and they took everything very seriously – signwriting the lorry, branding the show jackets, rugs, numnahs and so on. I still couldn't believe my luck, though, at having secured the backing of what was to become such a prolific company, but then Philip was very much a man of the moment, sponsoring people he believed in.

While it would have been easy for me to remain at the level I was – and make a reasonable living at it – investment by a big, bonafide company like Toggi equalled opportunity, the opportunity to climb that bigger mountain and set my sights on more testing shows, shows that involved more travelling, shows that may have been more difficult to win. With official backing came the promotion, the marketing of me: 'Tim Stockdale international showjumper'. But the sponsorship deal cut both ways in terms of what it also did for Toggi – I'd have a few more quid in my pocket to do the bigger shows and help create greater brand awareness for Toggi.

My vet, Thorsten Feddern, recommended that we saw Dovecote Farm – it was love at first sight and it was ideal for our requirements

The buildings were all in place but some needed renovating. Dad and I worked tirelessly on them – thankfully I've inherited his building skills and can lay a few bricks

The finished yard. Me and Laura are passionate about this place. It's been a labour of love for both of us

The Traxdata sponsorship
was announced in 1998 and
my lorry took on a new livery

I came second in a big class in
Gijon, Spain, on Traxdata Samoens,
so-called because his owner, John
Cosgrove, had a house in Samoens

When Glenwood Springs came to me, he had £286 on his winnings record. After four months, he'd won £23,000. Woody was a winning machine and is happily retired at home with us

Wiston Bridget was sharp, quirky and difficult to manage but so brave. I needed all my expertise to keep her on the straight and narrow, for she could bolt for Britain! Spookily, the field she was born in now belongs to my brother Ivan

I was selected with Parcival for the British team for the World Equestrian Games in Jerez, 2002 – the biggest competition of my career so far

I joined Fresh Direct in 2002 and have been sponsored by them ever since. Their chairman, Les Harris, is a huge supporter of showjumping

A chip off the old block – my eldest son, Joseph, on Miss Muffet

Fresh Direct Corlato (Ruby) came to me as a six-year-old. In our time together, I never once got the feeling she would ever let me down

Fresh Direct Animation was a solid horse and a reliable stand-in for me while Corlato was recovering from injury

My younger son, Mark, on Beauty –
laughing as always! Miss Muffet
(above right) was the perfect pony
for Joseph to learn on and gain
confidence jumping – a discipline
that's close to their mum's heart.
Laura (right) is seen here at Balcombe
Hunter Trials as a teenager

The only way is down! This is one of those hairy moments when you have to rely on your horse

I always felt that Fresh Direct Kalico Bay – seen here in 2007 – was a superstar but I never thought he'd fulfil my lifetime ambition

No words can describe how proud I felt representing Team GBR at the Beijing Olympics in 2008 on Fresh Direct Corlato

The British showjumping team finished fifth in Beijing and I came 16th in the individual final, the highest placed British rider. I was pleased with that

Chapter 15

Money makes the world go around

- Eating out of the gutter!
- R.E.S.P.E.C.T
- Toggi Samoens
- A horse called house

Even though I'd secured a fantastic sponsorship deal with Toggi and won a couple of lucrative shows in Portugal, the financial constraints of setting up on my own never seemed to ease and this hand-to-mouth existence was becoming the norm. The prize money was obviously an added bonus, because I still relied on my 'bread-and-butter money' from teaching for day-to-day living. Any extra I earned from winning a few competitions would go straight into my savings account or I'd use it to buy anything I needed for the horses.

I was also starting to sell the odd horse, but not without learning how to do it properly and I picked up some valuable tricks of the trade from a few of the dealers. I'll never forget one hilarious story I heard about an Irish dealer selling a 22-year-old horse, but passing it off as 11.

"Eleven and eleven he is, sir," he'd say, "eleven and eleven he is." Well, of course, 11 and 11 make 22…

The next couple of years were also about consolidation, being as consistent as possible and getting a few wins on the county show circuit, which I loved. My favourite county shows were

Royal Cornwall, Lincoln, the Royal Norfolk, Suffolk County and Royal Welsh, because I'd try to scoot off for a round of golf in-between classes. But Royal Welsh was also a favourite because of the commentator there. He was very annoying, but funny too, with his ridiculous catchphrase... "Latecomers will not be entertained." Now I know it sounds trivial, but he drove us all insane, because if we'd heard it once, we'd heard it a thousand times and it used to wear a bit thin being woken up by his voice so early in the morning.

"At 8.30am in ring one, we have the cobs. At 9.30am in ring two, there's the 14hh and under. At 10.30am in ring three, it's the working pony class..." he'd chatter... "We've been in touch with the police and all roads into the showground are clear, so latecomers will not be entertained."

I suppose it was funny because this guy obviously loved his job, and the thought of being in charge, of having the attention. However, to showjumper John Popely, he was beginning to sound like a cracked record.

"I'm fed up with this," said John, "being woken up at 7am every morning by that nincompoop. Tomorrow, I am going to cut him off. I'm going to snip his wires and disconnect his tannoys."

Sure enough the next day, as our pal started his spiel, John cut the wires and legged it back to the wagon. It was cruel, it was heartless, the poor guy's big moment had been scuppered. But we thought it was hilarious and sat in our wagon laughing till we cried. About an hour later, however, the showground surged back into life...

"There has been an act of vandalism, we know who you are and are coming with the authorities to arrest you." John was looking over his shoulder all day. But they didn't arrest him and it's one of my abiding memories of the Welsh Show.

The New Forest Show was another favourite of mine, because there was such a good, happy, almost carefree, atmosphere about the place, especially at night when a group of us would get together, have a few bevvies, indulge in a bit of banter and leg pulling, and discuss the events of the day – much the same as any bunch of lads enjoying a pint after work.

County shows always offered such memorable times and none more so than the barbecues Harvey Smith would prepare for us at the Royal Show. It had almost become a tradition and he loved to organise it for everyone, setting up a little fire with twigs and bits of wood he'd found in the hedgerows. In fact, that was quite a sight – Harvey Smith, one of the most famous showjumpers on the circuit, scrabbling around in the bushes and hedgerows looking for kindling, snapping off bits of twig here, there and everywhere. He'd emerge from the bushes looking bedraggled, dishevelled and with bits of hedge clinging to his sweater and tangled up in his hair. Harvey looked deranged.

But he was particular about his twigs, was Harvey. They had to be the right length, the right thickness and they had to be dry and any that he wasn't happy with would be discarded with a look of disgust on his face. And woe betide anyone who tried to tell him what to do. So while Harvey was making up the fire, the rest of us would disappear to the food halls on the showground to get a few sausages, a bottle of wine and a few cans of beer.

Harvey really enjoyed entertaining and he was very practical when it came to rustling up what raw materials he needed to build a barbie – he'd comb the showground for any old bricks lying around and he was extremely innovative when it came to improvisation. On this occasion, he'd set up his metal grille on a few bricks and once the fire was just right, and the embers had a healthy glow, we'd put our sausages on and sit around on straw bales waiting for the maestro to divvy up the spoils.

"You've done a great barbecue, Harvey, well done," I told him one evening as we all sat around the camp fire, savouring each delicious mouthful that he'd prepared lovingly. "It's delicious, mate, it really is, you've thought of everything as usual. Tell me, do you bring the grille with you to every show?"

"No, lad," he said, "I didn't bring the grille with me. I found it."

"Where did you find that then? It's perfect for the job."

"Well, that bit of grille there," he said, "was what was in gents' toilets, in the urinal gutter, but it's all right – I washed it first."

The grille Harvey had just cooked our sausages on was the

grate that was placed over the gutter to stop litter going in.

"It's fine, lad," he said when he saw our horrified faces, "it's been sterilised, it's been on the fire. Nowt wrong with it." No one could do a barbecue like Harvey...

He'd pitch up with all sorts of paraphernalia on his lorry, which he'd use for one thing or another – and I for one was intrigued by his ingenuity. He'd use upturned dustbin lids to feed his horses and instead of tying them to the side of the lorry, he'd tie their heads to their front legs, so they couldn't wander off. It probably sounds a bit odd, but it was a practical way of getting his horses out of the lorry for a bit of a leg stretch and a feed. He'd have three or four horses out, heads tied to legs, feeding out of dustbin lids – he was like a New Age traveller.

The County circuit was great fun but it also provided a good yardstick for measuring where you were ranked in the grand scheme of things. But then it was a lot tougher than today. You'd learn to jump with some top-level riders over some huge fences, and if it was chucking it down and the ground wasn't perfect, you'd just have to get stuck in, a case of do or die. The county show circuit alone was so unlike the streamlined nature of showjumping today – the fences were bigger and more solid, and it was a more brutal sport altogether. Excuses for under-performing were given very short shrift.

The circuit also taught me a few valuable lessons about house-keeping, in that you had to win to make it financially worth-while. Whenever I went to a show, for example, I'd write on the front of the schedule what it had cost for me to get there – entries, diesel etc. That focused the mind and if you were con-sistently good, you could actually make a tidy little sum out of the county shows. Six hundred pounds doesn't sound a lot in this day and age, but it was good money then and if you could take that sort of sum home after each show, you were laughing. In fact, I laughed all the way to the bank when I won £2,100 at the Royal Cornwall Show; I thought I'd scooped the jackpot.

I still try to do the odd county show when I can, as long as it doesn't clash with any of the competitions abroad, because when it comes down to it, there's no contest. The money abroad is better, as is the standard of jumping. It's a real shame that most of the county shows are now held at the weekend, because I'm sure they'd attract some of the bigger names if they were rescheduled for earlier in the week – as is the Great Yorkshire, which runs from Tuesday to Thursday – so that riders would still be able to compete in the internationals on the Continent at weekends. Having said that, I'd encourage any Young Rider to get out there on the county show circuit. It may be tough, it may be competitive, but there's no better platform for gaining experience.

Because I was so busy competing, however, it was easy to let the fundamentals slip – buying new horses and bringing them on, ready to replace old timers when they're retired and put out to grass. It's a time-consuming business, but trips to the Continent came with the territory and I'd travel to Europe probably once every two months in search of my next horse – not with anything specific in mind, other than the fact I was looking for my next showjumping superstar. While Toggi's sponsorship meant I had a bit more buying power, it's not as if I had a bottomless pit of cash. My shopping list would usually include a horse with talent, something with bags of potential and more often than not, a youngster to produce and bring on. With that, though, comes a greater risk because you're paying for a horse's potential rather than proven ability, so you never know for sure what you're going to end up with once you've trained it up – a superstar or an amateur's horse.

I'd meet up with a number of different agents who all had their contacts, but I wouldn't go to the same yard over and over again, because they started to know what I was looking for in the way of temperament and trainability and would miraculously have "just the horse for you". So I was careful not to give too much away – I wanted to keep the dealers fresh, to keep them thinking, to keep them guessing, a bit like prospective buyers do to me these days.

I remember one such trip to Germany, to a yard just outside Frankfurt. I'd been on the road all day looking at horses with a friend of mine, Shelley Redbardt (now Robert Smith's partner) and was beginning to get weary. It hadn't been a particularly successful day and nothing had taken my fancy – plenty of good-looking horses, but all just lacking that something special. By the time we arrived at this last yard, it was dark, pitch black and must have been 11pm. There was no one around other than the dealer who spoke no English – his name was Reinhold Distel. He had no staff at that time of night, so was running around tacking up horses himself, pulling them out, four or five of them. It was getting on for midnight when he led this magnificent chestnut horse into the arena. Reinhold had a very small indoor arena, the size of a postage stamp, in which there was room for only two jumps. This horse was phenomenal and still only six years old. I thought he was the best thing I'd ever sat on.

Next morning, my first call was to John Cosgrove. I told him all about the horse and said I'd love to buy him, having already structured a deal in my mind. I was so serious about this horse that I was going to ring my sponsor, Toggi, and ask for my sponsorship money in advance so I could buy him. When John heard this, it was the assurance he needed to come in on the investment and put up the rest of the money, two-thirds. He trusted my judgement that this horse was going to be a superstar and when we both went to Frankfurt the following week he, too, thought he was fabulous.

A couple of months or so before I bought the horse – Toggi Samoens (so-called because John Cosgrove had a house in Samoens, France) – Laura and I had become engaged and were saving up to buy a house of our own. So it was only right and proper that I let her know what I wanted to do. She was very supportive of my career and I was sure she wouldn't have any objection if I used our savings for the horse.

"Just remind me again, when are we going to get married?" she asked.

"When we buy a house, darling," I replied.

She laughed: "You know what your problem is don't you? You can't spell," so ultimately this horse became the horse called House.

The plan was still to get married, however, so spending our

money on a horse instead of a house was not some kind of ruse on my part to avoid tying the knot. Quite the opposite. We had clicked, right from the start. Laura would become my wife one day – of that, I was certain.

Chapter 16

Will you marry me?

- Getting engaged, finally
- New horsepower
- Tough at the top
- Filming 'Cutting Edge'

My proposal to Laura in 1995 could turn into a comedy farce if I wasn't careful. We were on holiday in St Lucia with Anna and Andy Austin, plus my brother Ivan and his girlfriend Lisa, now his wife. We'd been out to dinner and it had been a lovely evening, with my best mate and my twin brother in on the surprise I was about to spring on Laura. Everything was now in place for the most important decision of my life, asking Laura to take me on. It followed weeks of preparation that had been akin to a military operation. I'd already visited Laura's father, Tony, and he seemed pleased that I was taking his daughter off his hands —although at first he thought it was a ruse, that I wanted to see him to ask to borrow some money.

I'd kept the engagement ring hidden at home before transferring it to Ivan's suitcase the night before we flew to St Lucia — I couldn't have risked Laura finding it in my luggage which she could easily have done as she did all my packing for me then — and still does.

Just as we arrived back at the house after dinner with everyone, I nonchalantly asked Laura if she fancied a walk down to the beach where I'd planned to pop the question. Now this could have looked odd to the others, as we'd have to go back the way we'd just come from the restaurant. It might seriously have backfired, had it not been for the intervention of Ivan and Andy preventing Anna and Lisa from gate-crashing our romantic stroll.

"Oh, we'll come too!" they'd squealed in delight.

Just what I didn't need, my well-planned proposal looking dangerously close to heading for a burton.

After some careful distraction of the other ladies by Ivan and Andy, Laura and I crept out and strolled hand-in-hand down to the sandy beach, then sat at the water's edge in the moonlight. I'm not usually one for romantic gestures so I was pretty sure she would get suspicious after a while. I was nervous so that made me quiet and I'd had to think fast when she asked what I was up to, as I'd tried casually to manoeuvre her from one side of me to the other as we walked along. I had the bulky ring box in my pocket and didn't want her bumping into me in case she felt it against her leg, so I tried to switch her around. It was all a bit cack-handed, but I got away with it, I think.

"Will you do me the honour of becoming my wife?" I blurted it out in one anxious breath.

She stared at me, speechless, for what felt like an eternity.

"Of course I will," she replied.

We were so happy and couldn't wait to get back and tell everyone we were getting married. It was another exciting upward curve for me at home too, as people wanted to send me more horses. They weren't all superstars but there were some exciting prospects and I'd collected some really decent horses by this time – Toggi Samoens, owned by John Cosgrove; Toggi Oeillet, owned by Keith Doyle; and Toggi Interview, owned by a lovely lady called Gail McBride.

It was Andy Austin who first mentioned Interview to me. He'd ridden him as a novice some time before. I went to try Interview and liked him a lot. His owner at the time, Alison Begley, agreed to sell him to me and a city trader friend of mine, Stuart McBride, for £15,000 as she was going off to ride racehorses instead. A few days later, however, Alison pulled out of the deal.

I think she was very attached to the horse and couldn't face selling him when push came to shove. Stuart was quite disappointed as he'd intended the horse as a present for his wife, Gail. In fact, he was so disappointed that he decided to take legal action. I was reluctant, though, as taking someone to court over a horse seemed a bit extreme. People back out of selling their horses all the time for whatever reason.

Anyway, we went to see Stuart's lawyer in London and explained our case. The lawyer told us that we'd have grounds if we could prove that the seller intended to sell the horse, and for that we needed a witness to corroborate our story. Otherwise, it would simply be a case of their word against ours. In the end, we proved that there had been a verbal contract for sale as, quite innocuously, I'd asked my vet to phone the seller to arrange a vetting because I thought it would be easier than me relaying messages between them. The vet would, therefore, be able to act as a witness to the agreed sale. I had mixed feelings about us pushing the sale through like this but, at the end of the day, a sale had been agreed upon and I wanted the horse, as did Stuart. Things were tense between us and Interview's previous owner for a while but when he retired after a glittering showjumping career, he went back to them and we are now very friendly.

While we went to great lengths to ensure the purchase of Interview, he was not, ironically, a horse who endeared himself to me because he went in such an individual style – he ran at his fences. I didn't really like riding him because he made me break the rules of my style. I couldn't ride him in a nice rhythm or he would just knock all the jumps down. Don't get me wrong, he was a prolific horse and he won a lot of good classes but he wasn't exactly a joy to ride unless it was chucking it down with rain. If he had to jump out of 3ft of mud, he made a better shape over the fence as it slowed him down and gave him more time to use himself properly, even though it also meant he had to put in more effort to get over it. He was as brave as a lion, though, so nothing fazed him. And to be fair, he won good money and was a really useful addition to my string.

I'd also taken on a horse called Sànta's Echo, owned by Mr and Mrs Chubb. I was surprised to find what a wilful little character Santa's Echo was when he came to me. He was a wily horse of Irish breeding and had been imported as a youngster by Jimmy Lister. He was a comical little so-and-so and I soon discovered that he had a real will of steel and when he didn't want to do something, there was no way on earth you could make him. So I would let Santa believe he was running the show and allow him to run on a bit and jump, almost out of control, as much as I dared because the fences were big. The rounds weren't pretty, but you had to let him do his own thing. I just wouldn't try to force him, whether it was trying to get him over a water jump at which he'd stop once in a blue moon, load into the lorry or walk into the wash box. He was like a petulant child and if he ever said no to you, you didn't stand a chance.

However, he was a prolific winner, picking up eight Grand Prix titles – five of those in one year alone, including Lisbon and Royal Windsor. Santa was the first horse with whom I was short-listed for an Olympic Games – Atlanta in 1996 – and I have been short-listed for every Olympics since. Santa came along just at the right time, when Mighty McGuigan was starting to suffer from lameness issues and was looking to retire, so he quickly became my top horse.

Not only were there some really competitive riders on the international circuit, there were also some really prolific winners – we were all vying for the main prize after all. However, the one really determined character who stands out for me was Austrian rider, Hugo Simon. Now he may have only been little in stature, but he was big on competitive spirit. We were both competing at Olympia and Hugo had had a really successful show, winning four or five good classes. We were both riding in the Grand Prix and I remember being clear until the last fence when Santa's Echo had one of his occasional moments and stopped, kicking the marker number by the side of the jump. The judges heard this and rang the bell to signal a fence rebuild. Then one arena party ran across to look at the fence, saw that nothing had been dislodged, put his hand up to signal the clock to start running again, then I jumped the last fence and went through the finish.

"So that's three faults for Tim Stockdale," announced the commentator over the PA system. "But we have to add six seconds for rebuilding the fence and I'm afraid that puts Tim out of the time allowed, so he's actually got two time faults, making a total of five faults." But I hadn't knocked anything down...

I objected to the ruling, explaining what had happened. So after the judges played back my round on the video, it was announced that because I hadn't hit anything and nothing had been dislodged, the six seconds were deducted and I was inside the time allowed, so I walked away with just three faults for the refusal. There were nine clear rounds and I came 10th, for which I won £1,000 but Hugo Simon, who was on four faults, put in an official complaint. He was one of six other riders who were sharing a pot of £1,000 and due to get £165 each.

"It is wrong, it is wrong," he ranted, "you should not be getting the money, you hit the fence." He was having none of it and wouldn't listen to reason when I explained what had happened.

"Hugo, I didn't hit the fence, I didn't dislodge anything. The judges made a mistake and they've rechecked the video. I've won my money fair and square."

Still he went on at me, screaming that it wasn't fair. He'd just banked about £25,000 at that show and was trying to stop me getting my £1,000. We were only inches away from each other growling like a pair of caged lions. It was Eddie Macken who came to the rescue. Sensing my frustration, Eddie pushed past and squared up to Hugo. "Let me tell you something, Hugo," he said. "This lad needs £1,000 more than you need £150, lay off him." And with that, Hugo backed off, still muttering that life wasn't fair... Things were probably said in the heat of the moment and I'm sure Hugo believed what he was saying, but it taught me how fiercely competitive this business can be.

In the New Year, I was approached to do a programme about showjumping for Channel 4's 'Cutting Edge' series. The approach had been made through the BSJA's marketing department and the programme was to be a behind-the-scenes look at showjumping featuring me, Rastafarian showjumper Oliver Skeet, Emma-Jane Mac and some of the organisers within the sport. Admittedly, some people in the industry had reservations about the project, but I felt I had nothing to be worried about and nothing to hide.

"Just be honest, be yourself," John Cosgrove had advised. "If you go ahead with it, not only will it raise the profile of Tim Stockdale Limited, it will give your sponsors a lot of mileage."

So I agreed to do it and threw myself headlong into the world of television. It was filmed at my yard in Chesham, and turned into days and days of camera crews and re-filming. Then about three-quarters of the way through filming my story, the series started airing on Channel 4, kicking off with Moor Park Golf Club in north London. When I watched the first episode, it horrified me. Canny editing made some of the old duffers look like cantankerous old farts surrounded by eccentric, middle-aged women, all pompous, rude and opinionated. It didn't bode well.

On the strength of this, tremors of uncertainty rippled through our industry, especially me, as I was concerned that we'd come over as a bunch of numpties, so I began to wonder if it was going to cause more harm than good. What didn't help the situation, either, was the fact that the BSJA marketing department, who'd got me involved in the first place and made all the introductions, made a 180-degree turn. When I needed reassurance that what I was doing was sensible, they couldn't give it to me.

As a result, I told the film company I needed a week to think the project through. To be honest, I couldn't come up with a good enough reason to pull out. I thought about John Cosgrove's advice to "be yourself". They couldn't take a side-swipe at me or distort the character if I didn't pretend to be anything other than myself – outspoken, to the point and honest. I was simply going to demonstrate how difficult the sport can be, how hard I had to work to be successful, how hand-to-mouth the business was and that I was just a normal guy wanting to be a showjumper. What was there that could be misconstrued?

John Cosgrove stood behind me, guided me, and I decided to continue with the programme. It turned out to be one of the best things I ever did because, although 'Cutting Edge' did not go down a storm in certain equestrian circles, a lot of people in the industry commented on how normal and down to earth I seemed and how interesting it was to see the other side of the business. So all things considered, I think I came out of it pretty well.

Oliver Skeet, supposedly Britain's first black showjumper, also agreed to be included in the programme, because he was on a massive promotional trip at the time, taking advantage of all sorts of marketing opportunities that came his way. Although I'd been reported in the press as saying that "Oliver Skeet was just another rider with a funny hairdo", I liked him a lot because he was true to himself. He was only in it for the short term and the moment that people realised he couldn't compete on an equal footing with the big guns, he was sunk. I remember reading a newspaper article about him which said something along the lines of, 'When most showjumpers were on the playing fields of Eton, Oliver Skeet was stealing his first car in Brixton'. The truth of the matter was that he'd never stolen a car in his life and it's well documented that some showjumpers haven't even been to school, let alone been on the playing fields of Eton. How wrong could they be?

What 'Cutting Edge' did teach me was how clever television companies can be with their editing, manipulating a subject to put exactly the spin they want on a programme. It was, however, a good lesson for me and I realised that I had to be sharp, on the ball and not get caught out with tricky questioning. More importantly, though, I began to realise the value of publicity and firmly believe that up-and-coming riders today should grab every similar opportunity they get to market themselves. Effective promotion is a valuable asset.

Chapter 17

Home is where the heart is

● Humiliation in front of Luciano Pavarotti
● Buying Dovecote Farm
● Wedding bells
● Honeymoon disaster

One particularly memorable moment, for all the wrong reasons, was when we were selected to compete in the Nations Cup at Modena, Italy, in 1996, at the world-famous Pavarotti International in front of one of my heroes, Luciano Pavarotti, a renowned horse lover. True to form, on the first day, Santa's Echo decided he wasn't really in the mood for jumping and wouldn't go near the water (shades of Andy Austin and Orthos at Royal Windsor), so I was eliminated. I then heard that Nick Skelton was not going to be jumping Showtime in the Nations Cup the next day, because he wanted to save his horse for the £50,000 finale class. Regular Chef d'Equipe, Ronnie Massarella, responded: "Well, we'll have to jump Stockdale then."

The next day, I entered the arena as the last to go for Great Britain in the first round. We jumped the first five fences clear, then were about 50 metres away from the water jump when Santa slammed on the brakes. I managed to inch my way closer to the water's edge, donkey kicking every stride of the way for the little good it did. So I turned him away and tried to get more of a run-up – but no luck. We had more of the same, taking an age to get anywhere near the water. I must have looked ridiculous, like a complete novice out for their first jumping lesson. And then I spotted Ronnie waving frantically.

"Ride him through it, ride him through it," he gesticulated wildly to me.

What did he think I was trying to do? I knew I had to get him through it, even if it just meant walking him through it. I would be eliminated as this was my third attempt. So I kicked and shoved, with arms and legs flapping, feeling a complete buffoon on live Italian TV – and in front of Pavarotti as he watched from his private box. It was a full-blown 'Thelwell' moment if ever there was one. They finally rang the bell signalling my elimination so I took the walk of shame, ashen-faced, out of the arena.

"I tried to ride him through it," I said to Ronnie, "but I just couldn't get him anywhere near it."

"I was telling you to come out, you silly sod," he said, "I could see you weren't going to get anywhere," he explained.

After all that fuss, I was mortified when Simon Brooks-Ward came up to me, stony-faced. "Tim," he pronounced, "the Maestro wants a word with you. Come to his box now." The 'Maestro' was, of course, the great Pavarotti.

My heart stopped, I felt flustered, tiny beads of perspiration prickling my forehead at the shock. This is going to be the ultimate humiliation, I thought, banned from the showground by Luciano Pavarotti himself. How could I live this down? He'd understand that my horse was being wilful, surely? It's what any rider in a similar situation would have done. My mind was racing as I started the long climb up the stairs to his box.

"I can't believe what you've just done, Tim," said Simon, which only made matters worse. My mouth was dry, I was speechless, I'd been stunned into silence – which doesn't happen often.

"You know that Pavarotti loves horses, Tim, and you've just ridden yours like that, trying to make him walk through the water. Whatever were you thinking?"

"Well, I thought Ronnie was telling me to ride through it," I said, garbling out my explanation. I felt wretched, dreadful –

this was what it must feel like going up to the gallows. I followed Simon up the stairs and just as we got to the top, Simon, his hand on the doorknob, turned and burst into laughter, obviously not able to contain himself any longer. Then he looked past me to the bottom of the stairs to where Ronnie Massarella, Nick Skelton and all the other British team lads were standing, doubled up laughing. The rotten pigs had set me up. I'd been had.

After they'd managed to pull themselves together, the other three members of the team – William Funnell, James Fisher and Di Lampard – each jumped clear in the second round, which meant that I didn't have to jump again. And so we won the Nations Cup but at the press conference afterwards the first question was: "Why did you jump Stockdale?"

My response to that hurtful jibe came later, at the Maubeuge Grand Prix where I won my weight in wine. I'd been going to Maubeuge for a couple of years before taking Santa there but on this particular day, he jumped fantastically well. The show is held in the middle of town and the hotel where the best riders and Grand Prix winners stay is right next to the arena. On the day of the Grand Prix, having jumped clear in the first round, I sat and watched Nick Skelton go into the lead with Showtime and thought, 'I can beat that'. I said to the girl who was grooming for me at the time: "Right, let's show them. We're gonna get this thing won."

I think I beat Nick's time in Maubeuge by about one second to claim the Grand Prix victory as well as the Leading Rider prize – my own weight in fine wine. I was placed on one side of some medieval scales while they balanced up the other with cases of plonk. Not weighing much in those days, I hooked my fingers under the ledges of the platform to try to hold myself down as they piled the wine on. But it backfired catastrophically when my fingers became trapped, taking the weight of a truck load of wine and additional crates of champagne. It was agony.

Another memorable win for me and Santa that year was in Jerez, Spain, and I flew Dad over for the final Sunshine Tour

Grand Prix. Santa won it in style, but as I stood there during the prize-giving, as the National Anthem played, I noticed that a scuffle had broken out. My dad is fervently patriotic and as the anthem started, he had obviously stood up. But a couple of Spanish guys in front of him remained seated and were chattering away. So Dad grabbed them by the scruff of the neck, pulled them up to their feet, oblivious to the stream of abuse in Spanish, and held on to them until the anthem finished. I was so proud of him that day for doing that.

Fresh from my wins on the Continent, I came home and won the Grand Prix at Royal Windsor, again with Santa. My philosophy changed slightly, along with returning good fortune. I had always entered every class to win it, but was now thinking about the bigger picture and producing my horses for targeted shows, rather than taking them out and jumping at any and every available opportunity.

Money was a big influence at this point because I'd earned more in my first three Grand Prix wins of 1996 than I had in the whole of 1995. But in order for my top horses to be at their best, they needed to be rested more and kept fresh for the big competitions. It's a risky ploy if you then have a fence down, but a risk worth taking as far as I could see. I also had to think about our new home, which was going to put a huge strain on our finances...

I was still running my business out of Lye Green Farm in Chesham, Buckinghamshire, when I received a call from my vet, Thorsten Feddern. He'd phoned to tell me about a yard in Roade, Northamptonshire, that he thought we should look over. We were now a bit overcrowded in Chesham and I'd been getting itchy feet for some time, and was keen to buy my own yard. So Laura, Dad and I went to have a look at the place.

When we arrived, we turned into the private drive, passed through a wide, open set of old wooden gates and parked in the middle of the purpose-built yard. We sat in silence as we scanned the property, speechless at what was on offer. It looked ideal, with its big indoor school, stables, a barn and a nice brick-built house. But that wasn't all.

As we were shown around the yard, it all seemed too good to be true. The property included two houses – a 16th-century, six-bedroomed house with a lake, beautiful gardens, and six brick-built stables in the prettiest courtyard setting. Attached was more accommodation consisting of a four-bedroomed flat on the top level and four single rooms of staff accommodation on the ground floor – and each storey with separate access. There was also an office, changing room with toilets and a tack room. The main yard had 12 boxes and featured an indoor school, complete with grandstand gallery and its own tannoy system. There was an outdoor school with a bark surface that had seen better days and 28 acres of land with its own cross-country course. The downside was the need for some serious renovation; but that only made me want it more as I could picture myself with my arsenal of power tools, bringing the place up to scratch.

I contacted the estate agent and John Cosgrove, as I wanted a second opinion. John thought we'd be mad not to buy the property. But it was on the market for £550,000 and that was the problem. However, because I was only interested in the commercial equestrian unit, not the main, manor house, the agent intimated that the property could be split. The place was called the Abbot-Davies Balancing Rein Centre and had been designed and built by Major Peter Abbot-Davies, who had imported the rein system from India.

The bottom line, though, was that I couldn't afford to buy the entire estate, so I made an offer on the equestrian unit. It was turned down, because they'd decided not to split the estate into two lots after all. I was disappointed to say the least, because this was a fantastic property with bags of potential, so not wanting to miss out completely, I made an offer for the whole lot of £470,000, only to be refused again.

I thought this was the end of it until 11 months and three weeks later – not that I was counting – when I received a phone call from the estate agent asking if I'd still be interested in purchasing the property at the price I'd originally offered. Of course I was, but they told me I'd have to complete on the purchase in three weeks.

It actually took three months to complete by the time I'd got the finance in place; and then I had to find a buyer pretty damn quickly for the other half, as there was never any question of being able to afford mortgage payments on the whole property. Luckily I did and sold the manor house with its lake, six stables and eight acres for £250,000 to a lovely couple called the Wisbey-Browns. The deal was done just 30 seconds before I bought the equestrian unit – it was all a question of the order of signatures. Talk about cutting it fine, but we were all delighted that everything had slotted into place at the eleventh hour.

Thinking about strokes of good luck, this was one of them. If Thorsten hadn't been called out to an emergency on the yard to stitch a horse who'd cut himself, then phoned us to tell us the place was for sale, we wouldn't be at Dovecote Farm today. And it has so many advantages. Not only is it ideally situated for travelling, but the buildings were all already here, although some were derelict and needed to be renovated. We are passionate about this place and developing it has been a real labour of love for both of us.

How Laura and I managed to find the time to get married still remains a mystery to us, for the day we bought Dovecote Farm, 6 July 1996, was the day we took on a whole heap of work to get the place up and running as quickly as possible. Consequently, our wedding day four months later became just another entry in the diary – albeit an important one. We'd been up to our eyes and ears renovating the house and the yard, so it's a wonder we didn't walk down the aisle covered in paint, because that's all we seemed to do from the day we moved in – paint, build and hammer in nails. It was endless, but satisfying, as our home and business gradually started to take shape.

We tied the knot on 16 November 1996 in Turners Hill, West Sussex, where Laura's parents lived and it was one of those wonderful winter's days – bitterly cold, but sunny and with brilliant blue skies. The wedding all went according to plan and the day is etched in my memory for all the obvious reasons.

The reception was quite a grand affair, held in the circular ballroom at the Effingham Park Hotel, West Sussex, where about 200 guests showed up to join in the fun before we flew off on honeymoon the following morning. Our destination was America, courtesy of showjumper John Popely's dad who, as a wedding present, had given us the use of an apartment he owned in Florida. While it was wonderful to get away for a fortnight, we were kidding ourselves if we thought it was going to be a restful couple of weeks, having worked flat out on Dovecote Farm right up until the wedding. We were still so charged up and both knew that after being so full-on with renovation projects on our new home, there was no way either of us could cope with sitting on a beach doing absolutely nothing – it just wasn't going to happen. So the first week of our honeymoon was spent enjoying the Disney experience, having a mad few days doing all the rides and kids' stuff before flying on to Antigua for a week of relaxation and downtime at a friend's house. It was a welcome opportunity for us to be together, away from the pressure and hubbub of the yard, to recharge the batteries, soak up the sun and play a bit of golf, one of Laura's favourite past-times.

"Just think," Laura said, as I was about to sink the winning putt on the last green, "we'll be on that flight tomorrow…" I think she was trying to put me off.

I looked up to see a British Airways jet soaring high into the brilliant azure sky, rising steadily in its climb away from the island. We watched until it was no more than a spec on the horizon and then it disappeared from view.

Only it wasn't tomorrow, it was today and that soaring silver bird taking British holidaymakers back to the UK should have been taking us back to Blighty too. Poor Laura had mixed up the departure days, thinking that we were flying home on Sunday. She'd got the dates wrong and she was devastated, crying her eyes out and inconsolable. But her dad, Tony, came to the rescue as he was working for British Airways at the time, so made a few phone calls and helped organise flights home for us. A useful father-in-law – now there's a first!

Chapter 18

Success breeds success

- The end of Santa's Echo
- Renovating Dovecote Farm
- A life lesson
- Going Greek

I had such a good run of great wins at international shows that year, none more so than Santa's last, great victory at the Mechelen Grand Prix towards the end of 1996. The course was big and technical and he performed like a star to beat of some of the best horse and rider combinations in the world. But shortly afterwards, he damaged a tendon pretty badly, having had a history of such injuries. Santa was 15 by this stage and had done a fantastic job for me, but after a year off and careful rehabilitation, it was clear he wasn't going to recover fully so was retired.

I was gutted to see him leave my string. With Mighty Mc-Guigan retired in 1995, Santa's Echo now gone and the sparkle that had surrounded me following 'Cutting Edge' fading fast, I could feel the rollercoaster heading for a downward curve. It was quite an uncertain time for me when I realised that the only horse I had coming through the ranks was the young, inexperienced Samoens. Fortunately, Interview had really stepped up to the mark that year as he won the Royal Norfolk Grand Prix and was placed third in the Hickstead Derby – I was lucky he was such a versatile horse. However, it was when I lost Santa's Echo that it really hit home how important it was to always be producing novice horses to replace the ones at the top.

All my hopes were pinned on Samoens now, even though he still needed mileage at the top level before he was ready to replace Santa. I wanted to take my time with him and do it properly. He was all I had and I didn't want to rush him and ruin him. I was realising more and more the importance of producing my young horses slowly and with care. I personally don't think the Young Horse classes in the UK are that useful for producing a top horse, so I don't focus on them. They encourage riders to do too much too soon with their horses. I would rather take my six or seven-year-old to an international show at St Gallen or Rotterdam and ride them around to get them used to it. If the classes are too big when I get there, I'll just ride them in the prize-giving and let them have a look at everything. I think that's much more useful than galloping a seven-year-old around.

I was very selective about the international shows I did with Samoens in 1997, partly for his benefit but also because I couldn't really afford to go trucking around the big European shows. As a nine-year-old, Samoens did win two Grand Prix events on that year's Sunshine Tour and I was excited about his future. Samoens was my next up-and-coming star, but Interview was my workhorse, so he jumped anywhere and everywhere that year, winning a lot of classes.

In the meantime, I found that people were keen to see me work with my horses, so I became more involved in presenting lecture-demos. I really began to enjoy them and the audiences seemed to like what I had to say. Over the years, I have done a number of 'tours' and shows with the likes of Leslie Law, Blyth Tait, Emile Faurie and Graham Fletcher, as well as young riders I've taught. They can be really good fun and, of course, they're quite lucrative which was just as well because I needed to finance the work we were putting in to the renovation of Dovecote Farm.

Offers to buy Samoens would also come along from time to time, but he was my best horse and if I sold all the silver, what would I be left with? I threw myself into building the yard, house and business, and went over to Europe a couple of times a month looking for young horses, both for myself and for clients.

Despite having a bit of a dry year, I still qualified for Olympia which I was really pleased about, as it's one of the best shows in the calendar. My favourite show, however, is Aachen – it's pure, raw showjumping and it has a unique atmosphere. The crowds are expectant, already buzzing when you walk all the courses for the day, as they don't rebuild and re-walk between classes. Plus, the jumps always seem so much bigger at Aachen – massive and imposing. Everything is run with military precision, on time and on schedule. Very Germanic. I love it there.

Spruce Meadows, Calgary, in Canada is my second favourite because, conversely, it's everything that Aachen isn't. Yes it's big and tough, but it has a softness about it that's really endearing. When you pull up at the competitors' entrance, there's a sign that says, 'Welcome to the athletes' and everyone is so helpful and smiley. Olympia is a close third, with its Christmas party atmosphere. It's the reward for top riders at the end of the year, so if you're in the top 10 you automatically get an invite. I have only missed out on an Olympia invitation twice in the last 20-odd years, once through injury in 2011 and the other because my place was given to Liz Edgar.

In 1992, one of the top 10 British riders pulled out due to injury. I think I was number 11 on the ranking list and Liz was 12, so by rights I should have had the invitation. I remember being really excited about going as it would be my first time competing there. I heard subsequently that Liz had secured the place, so I phoned Raymond Brooks-Ward who ran the show.

"Why have you invited Liz? She's below me on the ranking list, it's not fair."

"No, it's not fair," he'd replied. "You're absolutely right. But Everest Double Glazing puts an awful lot of money into showjumping and Liz is sponsored by them. You, my dear fellow, don't put any money into showjumping. So with the greatest respect in the world, if I have the option of Liz Edgar or Tim Stockdale at my show, the choice is clear."

I can honestly say I didn't feel bad about it or hard done by after speaking to Raymond, because he broke it to me like a man. He didn't bluff his way through a feeble excuse, he just told me like it was. He'd explained the commercial aspect of the decision and it made sense. Raymond was essentially saying to me, "Life isn't fair, so you better come to terms with this, young man" and he was right. But when I qualified for Olympia in my own right at the wild card competition a few weeks later and received my official invitation, he was the first to ring up to congratulate me. I had a lot of respect for Raymond Brooks-Ward, he did a lot for showjumping and was a great person.

Over the years, I've taken on a few pupils for intensive training, something I'd started at Lye Green Farm. One of the first and most memorable of those pupils had been a lovely Greek lad called Alexandros Georgiou, whose career was understandably encouraged by his mother, Forfor.

Now, the family came with a bit of a reputation. I'd heard a few things about them before I agreed to take Alexandros on, namely that his mother was very passionate about the sport and extremely demanding when it came to her son. Alexandros, on the other hand, was very laid-back about the whole thing. His mother's antics just seemed to amuse him more than anything. Forfor was the archetypal pushy parent. Every morning at nine o'clock, the phone would ring and I knew it would be her.

"Good morning, Tim, eet iss Forfor. How are you?"

"I'm fine thank you, Forfor, how are you?" I would say. Then I would brace myself because I knew what was coming next.

"I am VEEERRRY disappointed, Tim, veeerrry disappointed."

She would then launch into a tirade about what was wrong with her life, the horses, her son, everything. But mostly she felt the core problem lay with Alexandros and that I clearly wasn't doing enough to help him.

"Now, for my boy, you must get these horses to jump the clear rounds," she would tell me.

"But it's not as easy as that, Forfor," I'd tell her.

"Everybody I speak to, they say eets not difficult. You Tim, you Tiiiimmmmm, you must do this for him."

I'd get at least three phone calls a day from Forfor and it was persistent, whether she was extremely disappointed that Alexandros wasn't going well or delighted that he'd been selected for something big.

Forfor would invariably threaten to buy even more horses when she spotted one that took her fancy and was doing well, so keen were they to support their son. They certainly spent quite a pretty penny over the years when you take into account the horses, livery costs and my training fees. She expected me to travel whenever and wherever Alexandros was competing, regardless of whatever else was taking place in the showjumping calendar. The world and his wife had to drop everything for Forfor.

Subsequently, I was instructed to be at the European Championships in Cortina, Italy, to teach Alexandros who was on the Greek Young Riders team. His sister, Tatiana, who was based in Athens, was on the Junior team and was being helped by her trainer, a little, wizened old man who couldn't have been a day under 75 and looked a little like Yoda from 'Star Wars'. So it was a double whammy for the Georgiou family and Forfor was on hand, proud as punch, to preside over her children's training.

The atmosphere was tense as Forfor barked instructions to her kids. Her fury was unleashed like a caged, wild animal when Tatiana's trainer put up a practice jump that she thought was too big for her. Tatiana was a competent rider, like her brother, but on this occasion as she cantered in to the fence, she misjudged the stride completely, probably distracted by her mother's squawking. Her horse hit the back rail, turned over and pile-drove poor Tatiana into the dust. He heaved himself up and stood there with his leg swinging – not broken, but certainly injured and unable to jump for the championship. At this, Forfor went ballistic, venting her fury on the trainer.

Later that day, Forfor was driving back to the hotel when she came across the old trainer walking along the track. She floored the accelerator and aimed her car straight at the man, who was standing there with eyes on stalks, not believing what the hell was going on. As the car lurched forward towards him, sand spraying everywhere as she sped in his direction, he instinctively hurled himself into the ditch, bravely peering up to see the damage. He needn't have worried, however, because Forfor had obviously thought better of knocking the old guy flat and swerved at the last minute to avoid him. Obviously this was her idea of a joke, but then who knows what was going on in her mind?

Now fully aware of Forfor's likely reaction should anything else go wrong, it certainly put me on my toes and only went to confirm my opinion of this hot-blooded lady. Nations Cup day at the championships was a very tense affair and quite a big thing for these kids. Alexandros was the first man to go for Greece and he was absolutely terrified. I had done my best to settle him and the horse in the practice arena, but he surprised us all by riding an immaculate clear round with just one time fault. Forfor was ecstatic, over the moon, beaming from ear to ear and chattering away about what a wonderful job I had done. I was going to get a bonus she told me. Fantastic, I thought.

She was still busy smothering me and Alexandros with kisses when the second Greek rider went into the arena and had 12 faults. Excellent – Alexandros was still the best score. Not exactly a sportsman-like thought to be having in a team event, but it would make Forfor happy. Then the third Greek rider went round for eight faults. Things were still looking good. By this point, Forfor couldn't control her enthusiasm and she was positively bursting with pride. Not only did her son jump a perfect round, but was going to be the best Greek rider in the team. What more could a proud mother want? All her birthdays and Christmases were rolling into one before her very eyes. Then the fourth Greek team member went round, a girl who could really ride. Lo and behold, not only does she jump clear, but she's not had a time fault. Damn it.

Forfor stood up, swung around to face her son and screamed at the top of her voice: "Alexandros, you malaka, you malaka!". She then proceeded to cuff him round the ear, whereby he stumbled to the ground. The poor kid was completely taken by surprise as he sprawled helplessly on the floor, his immaculate riding clothes covered in dust and his mother standing over him like a raging bull. Not surprisingly, this didn't do a lot for the lad's confidence so he had two fences down in the second round and was greeted by Forfor yelling at him as he came out.

Although Alexandros did manage to pull himself together and go on to compete in the World Championships later in his showjumping career, he eventually escaped from the industry to become an equine osteopath. Looking back, I didn't charge the Georgious enough to keep their horses with me, I should have been getting danger money!

Chapter 19

I am not indestructible

- Traxdata
- Crashing down to earth
- Super-human healing
- Glenwood Springs

By 1998, I was starting to get invited to better shows – Maastricht in the Netherlands and Wiesbaden in Germany, for example – where you mixed with the cream of the sport and could earn tens of thousands of euros in prize money. I began doing a lot more shows in northern Europe and I enjoyed them, not just for the obvious earning potential, but also because they were well organised, professional and had a great atmosphere. This was where I wanted to educate Samoens and where I could learn a lot, especially in Germany and Holland. The courses suited me better.

It was around this time that Philip Billington decided to sell Toggi so my sponsorship contract with the company came to a natural end. Obviously, I was sad that the partnership broke up because I had genuinely enjoyed my time with Toggi and got on well with Philip. At the same time, however, I was excited to see what might be around the corner. I was now in the market for a new sponsor and while it was scary to have lost a large chunk of income, I was quietly confident. In fact, it was through a mutual friend, Naomi Lewis, that I was introduced to Jeanette and Kevin Edwards, owners of Traxdata, a new company that made and sold recordable CDs and DVDs. It was an organisation very much on the up, thanks to the computer boom of that era. The owners were showjumping enthusiasts and approached me to be part of their team of riders. Needless to say, I leapt at the chance.

Kevin was an interesting character – he started out as a cabbie, and told everyone that he learnt about business from listening to the city gents he carried to and from the airport. Traxdata grew at lightning speed in the late 1990s and in a few years, I heard its revenues had risen from virtually nothing to hundreds of millions. Kevin liked fast cars and sprawling mansions. Luckily for me, his wife adored horses and showjumping. Traxdata got into the sport in a big way, sponsoring a team of riders – me, Peter Charles, Philip Spivey, James Fisher, Stuart Harvey – and a number of high-profile shows and classes. For a few years, showjumping was saturated with the competing logos of Traxdata. Its merchandise was everywhere, and the company certainly didn't do things by halves. It was a real boom time for showjumping sponsorship, just what the industry needed – and I for one was lucky enough to ride high on the wave, enjoying it while it lasted.

My mountain of ambition still needed climbing but Traxdata were prepared to provide me with all the ropes and ladders I needed to scale it. It felt great to be so looked after and pampered, when all the branded clothes and rugs turned up in that distinctive royal blue that matched the new paint job on the lorry. With this new influx of cash, I could afford to compete abroad much more which I was thrilled about.

Kevin and Jeanette were also keen to raise the company's media profile and that of their riders, so they hired a PR company to help with marketing and promotion. They were very active sponsors, always pushing me to get out there, be seen and win. It was excellent for me because I became even more aware of the importance of marketing within my sport. I really enjoyed doing the PR stuff as well.

I loved appearing on Channel 4's 'The Big Breakfast' with

Chris Evans, to help publicise Horse of the Year Show. Channel 4 arranged for me, Andy Austin and James Fisher to go on the show and jump the big red Horse of the Year Show puissance wall, on foot, in the garden of the studios. It was a crazy, but hilarious, stunt and we had a lot of fun doing it. We had to wear our competition gear and they gradually made the wall higher and higher until one of us crashed into it. I think Andy was the winner.

I also went on the BBC's 'Can't Cook, Won't Cook' with Laura. We were competing against Irish showjumper Erik Holstein and his sister, so it was Ireland versus Britain. I was the 'can't cook', Erik was the 'won't cook' member of the team, and I tried to make a sticky toffee pudding, but that didn't go well which isn't surprising. And I had no inclination to learn how to do it better either. After all, what's the point of me ruining good food when there are so many people around who can make a much better job of it than me? It's a well-known fact in the family that if Laura goes away, she leaves the fridge completely bare because she knows I'll never open it. I just live on takeaways, or go to the pub for dinner.

I had some great fun with Kevin and Jeanette. They loved their nights out. At the end of one evening, Kevin came up to me and asked: "What have you got planned for tomorrow, Tim?"

"Riding some horses, teaching. Why?"

"Do you fancy a game of golf?"

"Sure, sounds lovely."

"Meet me at my place tomorrow morning at 8am, and bring your passport." Passport?

So I turned up at Kevin's the next morning to find Peter Charles and James Fisher waiting, both looking baffled and slightly confused as to what was going on. We were even more bewildered when Kevin's car took us to Heathrow, to board a first-class flight to Barbados where we played a round of golf, stayed in a beautiful hotel, played another round of golf and then flew back on Concorde. It was one of the most surreal moments of my life and yes, it probably was a bit showy, but we had a fantastic time. It was incredible to see how the other half lived their jet-set lifestyle. Kevin could have easily spent that money on himself, but he chose to spend it on us instead. But just when I thought things were going really well, along comes another bloody accident to bring me crashing back down to earth in a heap.

I'd taken on a couple of young Dutch stallions owned by a lady up in Aberdeen, Sandra Lynn Cordiner. She had paid a lot of money for these horses, Ludwig H and Champagne H, and her dream was to set up a little stud to breed showjumpers. Sandra was a bus driver. She spoke Doric which was the local dialect and I couldn't understand a single word she said. In fact, it was easier to get her to write stuff down. Sandra was quite eccentric, but a very hard worker. For all I knew, her family may have been quite wealthy and she drove that big old bus just to get out of the house. Anyway, I accepted her horses for training and decided to take them to Hollowell in Northamptonshire, one of the first outdoor shows of the season and one I really liked.

In fact, as it was close to home, we'd often take the whole yard there – 13 horses for two days' jumping. It was like a works' outing. Sandra's two youngsters weren't competing until later on in the day, so they'd be up the front of the lorry waiting their turn, although we'd have a swap around about lunchtime, putting horses who'd jumped up the front and those who were yet to go at the back. But talk about making an entrance – we hadn't banked on the exuberance of one of her horses as we brought him out. He was full of the joys of spring, leaping around all over the place and snorting like a steam train.

We managed to get the other horses back on the lorry, but could we get this boy back on? He refused point-blank to budge, so I collared a passer-by to hold my two horses while I went up behind him to shoo him forward – huge mistake! He double-barrelled me, quick as lightning, with both studded back feet, each of his hooves making perfect contact with each of my knees. His studs cut straight through my breeches and flesh and I fell to the ground screaming and clutching my knees. Blood poured everywhere, and I crawled to a neighbouring ramp to get off the wet ground. I just lay there, while people ran about, not sure what to do. I was scrunched up, whimpering on the ramp, when a lady came up to me and said: "Excuse me, could you move? I want to load my horse." I could have throttled her.

Finally the ambulance arrived and I was bundled in out of the rain. I lay there in agony, my breeches soaked red from the knee down. Through the haze of pain, I remember Nick Skelton poking his head around the door.

"I'm his friend let, me in." The paramedics made way, and he just looked me up and down.

"You're f***ed, you are." And with that, he left.

When I arrived at hospital, they told me that part of my left knee was poking out through my skin, a compound fracture. My knee was shattered, smashed to smithereens but luckily the right leg wasn't broken, merely lacerated. Well, that was good news! But I knew I was in real trouble when they hooked me up to a drip as soon as they'd X-rayed me.

"Why are you putting a line in?" I asked.

"In case you need drugs," he said.

I knew then that I was going in for an operation. As it turned out, I had to have my whole knee rebuilt. Luckily my surgeon, Mr Crump, had previously worked on Formula One driver Michael Schumacher when he broke his leg at Silverstone, so I was in good hands. They built a metal structure in my knee – to be taken out at a later date – that allowed me to walk and the bone to grow back in the right places.

Afterwards, I was moved onto a general ward to recover. It was a miserable place, dark and depressing and I was stuck inside, climbing the walls. The guy in the next bed had been admitted after shattering both his heels, and his feet looked like two black footballs stuck on the end of his legs. It turned out that he'd had a few drinks one night and thought he could jump off his roof onto some concrete – idiot. He was a smoker and lay there shaking and crying, not because his feet looked ready to drop off, but because he was desperate for a cigarette.

Then one day, obviously unable to take it anymore, he

plopped out of bed and crawled along the floor towards the door in a desperate attempt to go out for a smoke. He managed to drag himself halfway to the lift, which was no mean feat, before the nurses got hold of him, stuck him in a wheelchair and took him outside, where he'd sit all day long, chain-smoking to his heart's content.

I have to admit that I'd enjoyed a cigarette, or two, in my time but that experience put me off smoking completely. I didn't want the evil weed ruling my life, as it did with that poor bloke.

I lay there in hospital for more than a week, thinking about a tour of Spain and Portugal I was planning to embark on in five weeks' time. But would I be well enough to ride then? I was determined, however, that I would be ready and became obsessed with getting better. So much so that when I was discharged, I decided to use a magnetic therapy pad we'd use for the horses on myself. After all, if it reduced their healing time, why shouldn't it help me? So I'd sit for hours at a time with this pad over my cast and my knee would get red-hot and itchy under the plaster. It was quite funny really, because my knee was full of metalwork. If I held the pad at just the right angle, I could feel the rods holding my shattered bones together vibrating in the magnetic field.

When I went back to have the cast checked four weeks later, I asked the medic to X-ray it.

"There's no point, it's too soon," he replied.

"Please X-ray it and you'll see," I said to him. So he did.

"You must have got the date of the accident wrong," he commented, "because the level of bone growth is incredible." Thankfully, I was allowed to have the cast off.

I can't say whether or not my miraculous healing was down to the magnets, but it was either that or I'm super-human! As they cut through the cast, I was already thinking about which horse I might sit on the next day. What I wasn't prepared for, however, was the lack of muscle control I had in my leg. Quite simply, the nerves that control the muscles had gone to sleep, so I'd need physiotherapy to get them working again.

And with that, all my optimism evaporated. I was meant to be riding in Spain in a week. How was I supposed to do my job? It was a harsh lesson, realising I wasn't invincible; and it was very sobering. The physiotherapy exercises they gave me were excruciatingly painful and I continued to 'cook' my knee with the magnetic pad. In he end, though, I made it to Spain, five weeks and three days after my Hollowell horror. I did need help getting on and off the horses and had to sit with ice packs on my knees in-between classes, but I made it to the shows. Samoens and Interview jumped well on that tour and earned good money, which was some reward for the uncertainty during recuperation.

I guess I'm a tough cookie, though, so it didn't take long before I was comfortably back in the saddle. Once the flesh wound had finally settled down, the knee didn't really bother me. Competition-wise, I had some great Nations Cup performances with Samoens that year in Gijon, Lisbon and Wiesbaden. I was still, however, looking around for other horses to back him up. I could do with another couple of top horses if I was to make the most of my Traxdata sponsorship. Luckily I didn't have to wait long because Glenwood Springs came along.

Kiwi Sharn Wordley, who was riding for local people, John and Sue Bosher over at Brackley, was jumping 'Woody' in a speed class when I watched him at Wales and West. He was a handsome horse and I liked the look of him over a fence. It transpired, however, that Sharn was leaving for pastures new, so I was asked to value the Boshers' string of horses. While there, I sat on a couple of them – Woody and Ivera M – and told John I'd take the two of them to jump myself and sell for him at no cost.

When Woody, then an eight-year-old, showed up in my yard a week later, he had £286 on his winnings record. After four months with me, he'd won a whopping £23,000. He was a winning machine. I still have Woody on my yard even though he's now retired. You'd think he'd enjoy being turned out and left to enjoy his retirement, but not a bit of it, because when he's out in the paddock, he hates it. For all that, though, he's such a lovely character and great for hacking out with the youngsters.

Although Woody was a touch on the small side, his jump was

consistent and neat. He was so careful that he rarely had a jump down. The only thing that really held him back was that he didn't like water jumps. In fact, he couldn't even clear a fence that was near one, yet he would try heart and soul for you over any type of course – ironic, really, as he has a severe heart murmur and would never pass a vet so it's lucky John and Sue never wanted to sell him.

I tried to cure Woody of his water phobia one winter when he was having some time off, by turning him out in the indoor school at night and leaving a water tray for him to think about. But when I led him in there, he wouldn't look at it, choosing to go and stand in the far corner. Next morning, when we went to get him, he hadn't moved an inch. There was a big pile of droppings and Woody standing facing the wall just as I had left him. I tried again for the next two nights, but still Woody wouldn't move from his corner once he was left alone with the water tray. After that, I stopped trying to change him and just avoided classes with water jumps so I could play to his strengths.

Ivera M, on the other hand, turned out to be quite a handful as she was a stroppy mare. I won a class with her in Gijon soon after I got her and when I went in for the prize-giving, she behaved like an angel. But when I tried to move away for the lap of honour, nothing. She wouldn't budge, so I gave her a bit of a shove. Still nothing. Everyone was waiting for me to lead the procession so I gave her a hefty boot and she reared straight up, leapt forward, then bucked until I came off. She galloped round and round the arena, rosette flying in the wind and her winner's rug hanging off the side, setting off all the other horses in the line-up while I just sat on the floor and observed.

Needless to say, I didn't keep her long. Another quirky mare was about to come my way, and I'd need all my skills and expertise to keep this one, Wiston Bridget, on the straight and narrow.

Chapter 20

Lady Luck smiles on me again

● I love Australia
● Bolting with Bridget
● Parcival
● Fatherhood

A year after I smashed my knee to bits, I went back into hospital to have the metalwork removed and was told to take three weeks off to recover. Laura and I took full advantage and booked a holiday to Australia. I remember it for a number of reasons – the sun, the relaxation, the places we visited. Most especially, though, because Australia was where Laura fell pregnant with our first child, Joseph.

When we got back from Australia, I arrived home to find Wiston Bridget in my yard. While we'd been away, Stuart Harvey – another of Traxdata's riders – had decided he didn't want to jump at the top level any more. Bridget and another top horse of Stuart's had been bought for him by Traxdata, so they wanted to relocate these two horses to one of their other riders. Originally, James Fisher had taken them both to try while I was away. He'd got on well with the gelding but when he tried Bridget, she proceeded to take off with him, at walk, around the school, wherever. No matter what James did, he couldn't stop or turn her. In the end, he jumped off her while she was still walking, handed her to the groom and said: "I'm done with this one, thanks."

He rang Jeanette Edwards and told her that the gelding was perfect for him and he'd be happy to take him, but thought I should have the mare. With that, Bridget – who was then around nine years old – was delivered to Dovecote Farm, waiting for my return from Australia.

Bridget is a Shire-cross and extraordinarily sharp in the mind, very quirky and difficult to manage. Her mind wasn't particularly supple, however, so if there was something she couldn't work out, she'd just walk through it. She was an accidental foal after her father – a young Holstein colt – got in with the next-door farmer's Shire mare. Spookily, the field she was born in now belongs to my brother, Ivan. He had no idea when he bought the house.

The first time I got on her, she duly took off with me at the trot. Never one to be put off by a difficult horse, I was up for the challenge and keen to teach Bridget to shorten her stride between fences. So I would build a short one-stride distance and jump it over and over – but she would bounce it every time. Her redeeming quality was her power. Bridget had a huge jump and could leap herself out of trouble most of the time. There was nothing she couldn't jump – she was fearless and would give anything a go.

Robert Smith once said to me that Bridget had been born 20 years too late. If she'd been around in the 1970s, she would have been a world beater, back when the poles were heavier and the jumps big, simple and imposing. That's why she was so good at Hickstead because of its imposing fences. To be honest, I put a lot of man hours into Bridget but, my goodness, she was worth it. It may have taken a lot of repetition to teach her how to do something, but we got there in the end and she eventually learned to put one stride in that short distance. It was the beginning of a great partnership for us.

Bridget took over from Samoens as my main Grand Prix horse – she jumped on Nations Cup teams; we were shortlisted for the Sydney Olympics; and she came second in the Hickstead Derby. She also went well in the King George V Gold Cup at Hickstead.

For all her problems and trickiness, Bridget was one hell of a horse. She was also popular with the public and had quite a fan base. And if there's nothing that the public loves more, it's a horse with character – just like everyone loves a grey. And as luck would have it, I was about to land myself a lovely grey horse as well.

In 1999, I met my long-standing owners, Ann and Colin Garratt. They were involved with the showjumping scene, had a few decent horses and thoroughly enjoyed being part of the industry. I was as surprised as anyone when they rang me up out of the blue and offered to buy me a horse. When I met them, I could tell straightaway that they were very nice, hard-working people who loved their horses.

"What kind of horse do you want?" I queried.

"Ideally, we would love a horse who would go to the Foxhunter final," replied Ann. "That would be a dream come true."

"You know that a top-class five-year-old will cost quite a lot, don't you?" I asked.

"Fine," Ann replied without a blink.

"They are not always easy to find," I said.

"Fine. We'll be guided by you."

They just wanted to buy me a horse. I was really touched, so I set out to find them one. I saw a lovely six-year-old stallion in Holland, but he was a bit more money than I wanted to pay. So I rang Ann up and asked if they wanted to come to look at him the following week.

"I can't do that," she replied. That's odd, had they changed their mind, I wondered?

"Okay, when would suit you?" I offered.

"I can't come. I don't have a passport."

"Sorry, what?" was my stunned reply.

"I've never been abroad," said Ann. "But if you like the horse, we'll buy it."

It felt quite a responsibility finding them a horse after that conversation. They clearly trusted me with their money and I didn't want to get it wrong. I went to try the stallion again on the way to a show in Maubeuge. Funnily enough, he was awful the second time I tried him. He was as bad the second time as he was good the first time – kicking out poles and calling to other horses all the time. I rang Ann that evening and her disappointment was clear. Also, the stallion had been grey and she had always wanted a grey. But that night I had dinner with James Fisher...

"I tried this horse today, it was awful," I told him.

"You should go and try this horse of David McPherson's," he said.

"It's only a seven-year-old, but it doesn't half jump."

I knew David well, so I phoned and arranged to go and try the horse on the way back from Maubeuge. Of course, I fell in love with the horse almost instantly – and he was grey. David told me he was taking him out to Royal Windsor and I could go to see him there. So I arranged to meet Ann and Colin at Windsor and told them to look out for a beautiful, young, grey horse being ridden by David McPherson.

They arrived to see David riding a grey in a 1.50m class in the main ring and he jumped a beautiful clear round. Ann said: "It can't be him, we came here to see a young horse and that's obviously a Grade A."

This was their introduction to Parcival and he was, indeed, the horse they'd come to see. They bought him there and then. Ann and Colin are very unassuming and understanding. I didn't realise how lucky I was at the time and it was all down to that one phone call. They have been very supportive of me ever since.

Parcival (Percy) had tremendous scope and power, and he was a delight to ride. He went straight into the big classes, the size of the fences never fazing him – in fact, he was jumping big classes as an eight-year-old. He was always destined for the top, although he was initially frightened of jumping water but once his confidence and knowledge grew, he became a fantastic water jumper.

Samoens, meanwhile, had enjoyed an unbelievable year previously and we subsequently got an offer from a US rider who wanted to buy him. We agreed to sell – I felt I'd taken him as far as I could. It was the right time to sell him and was a good business move that meant we could reinvest in more horses. Nevertheless, it was difficult saying goodbye, as I'd put a lot of time and faith into him and produced him from nothing to the winner he turned out to be.

To top off a fabulous year, I became a father for the first time in 1999, when Joseph was born in October. I was due to jump in Liege, Belgium, after Horse of the Year Show when Laura was close to her due date. She assured me she felt fine, so I left for the show early Thursday morning, making the long drive across to Belgium to meet the horses at the show that afternoon. Laura phoned me just as I reached my destination and told me she'd seen her specialist. They needed to get the baby out straightaway so they were inducing labour. She told me to stay on course, get to the show and she would call back in an hour when she knew more. I duly arrived at the showground and tried to focus on the job in hand. Just as I was preparing to get on the first horse, Laura rang to tell me things were happening.

I tracked down Billy Twomey and asked him to exercise my horses for me – I had Percy, Bridget and Woody with me. I said I'd be back in a day 'or so' to finish the show, but Dutch rider Leon Thijssen was not convinced: "Once Laura's had that baby, Tim, a horse show's the last place you'll want to be," he warned.

"Don't be silly," I retorted, "it's a baby – there's nothing I can do once it's out." So off I went.

I jumped in my car and drove back non-stop to the hospital, arriving at 2am Friday morning in a sorry state, having spent nearly 24 hours in the car. Once I arrived, I had no idea what was going on or what exactly was expected of me. Laura was very calm about the whole thing – she'd had enough painkillers to knock out a horse and kept drifting off to sleep, much to my nervous irritation. In fact, the baby finally popped out at 7.30am on the Monday. It turns out I could have stayed at the show and even got back in time! But joking aside, I'm so glad I was there, I wouldn't have missed it for the world.

I was quite unprepared for the rush of emotion I felt when I held Joseph for the first time, it was incredible. Nothing comes close to topping the birth of my sons – no sporting achievements even come close, nor will any future ones. Fatherhood is the defining role for me. This will sound strange to most people but the main criteria I had for naming my children was how they would look on a cricket scorecard. Joseph Thomas Stockdale, or J T Stockdale, would look great, so that's how he was duly christened.

I had the best time at Olympia that year proudly showing off my new baby – and Joseph turned out to be a lucky talisman for the new millennium. Our second glorious son, Mark James Stockdale, or M J Stockdale, came five years later, in 2004, causing equal havoc for me at a show.

Chapter 21

Out with the old

- A prospective Olympian
- The Riders' Club
- Strength to strength
- Meeting Ruby

The turn of the millennium felt like the start of great things for me. I had a new baby, great sponsors, the best horses I could wish for, and was short-listed for the Sydney Olympics with Bridget. What more could I want? Although the mare had a great 18 months with me, I was realistic about my chances of Olympic selection, as I thought there were better horses out there. I did start to buy into the whole Olympic fever, though, and I really started to feel the positive effects of being named on the long and shortlist for the Games.

But 2000 was a year of change. Ronnie Massarella stepped down as Chef d'Equipe of the international team at the start of the year, having presided over it for decades. Ronnie was a very special man and enjoyed global respect.

Although I missed out on a place at the Sydney Olympics – the eventual team comprising John and Michael Whitaker, Geoff Billington and Carl Edwards, with Di Lampard as reserve – I remained positive. There were plenty more irons in the fire. In a situation like this, you have to bury the disappointment, try to rebuild and move forward, and generally speaking I'm pretty good at that. So the highlight of the year for me was being invited to Spruce Meadows in Calgary, Canada, for what is now one of my favourite shows.

Those of us on the Olympic shortlist had been told that if we didn't make it to Sydney, we'd get to go to Calgary, and this would be my first time there. The arena at Spruce Meadows is a bit like Hickstead in that it's big and sweeping, so I knew it would suit Bridget – and it did. We won a good amount of money there. Bridget also did really well in the Hickstead Derby that year, jumping a double clear, but John Whitaker and 20-year-old Welham pipped me at the post with a faster jump-off time. I was gutted and came away wondering if I'd ever have a chance that good again. It would be great to add that piece of silverware to the cabinet.

For me, the Sydney Olympics had another key significance. A changing of the guard was occurring, with a new wave of riders breaking through the ranks. And this was encouraging for British showjumping in general. The trouble with sending your best-possible riders everywhere is that you don't allow other riders coming up behind to get vital experience jumping at the top-level shows. Essentially, you starve off the next level down. You're not investing in your future. It also prevents there being any real competition for places on the teams if you don't allow emerging horses and riders to have a go. Competition at the top is healthy – you don't get too comfortable and it pushes you to do better. I remember Ronnie Massarella once saying he would rather have John Whitaker on a donkey in his team than any other rider. I'm sure at the time Ronnie thought this was a great thing to say about one of his star riders. But it served to re-enforce the 'us and them' attitude that the rest of us were feeling and it was, quite frankly, disheartening. Also, it didn't inspire owners to invest in other riders.

Eventually, in the late 1990s, the inevitable happened. The selectors began looking around for international team riders and the top three weren't there, due to injury and/or a lack of horse power. There was no one ready to take their place, and as a nation we dropped away from the top of the sport – we were no longer world beaters. Gradually, however, the politics of showjumping in the UK began to change for the better – out with the old, in with the new. Part of that change involved Robert Smith and I forming The Riders' Club in order for us riders to have a political voice. The catalyst for this move came after Nick Skelton fell and broke his neck soon after Sydney. The talk was that he was going to retire from riding, so he'd be the new Chef d'Equipe. But rather than us accepting it as a foregone conclusion, we felt it was high time that the rest of the riders had a say in what was going to happen. So we rallied the troops together.

Ironically, Nick ended up coming on-board with us. While he was a main beneficiary of the old regime, I don't think the way things had worked for the last two decades had in any way been engineered by Nick, nor by John and Michael, for their personal gain. They had just reaped the benefits of how the sport had been run by the powers of their time. Now, rightly or wrongly, I wanted to be a part of the political process and have a say in how our sport was managed. All things considered, it was quite an exciting time, a new dawn.

While The Riders' Club lacks a notable driving force these days, it certainly served its purpose at the time and we got what we wanted at the end of the day. We were on the look-out for a new team manager to carry the sport forward – someone who'd look at the bigger picture and select riders on pure merit. We wanted someone who would be prepared to represent us riders in boardrooms and at meetings. I was very keen on getting Derek Ricketts. I hadn't ever met him, but he was the best man on paper. An experienced and respected rider himself – he'd won a World Championship gold medal – and was well-liked among the riders. Also, he'd been out of the sport for a while, so he had no standing affiliations with anyone in the governing bodies or any of the riders. He just seemed like a good, straightforward guy.

An unofficial riders' poll took place – the results of which we took to the BSJA, as it was still known then. We recommended Derek got the job. This put the BSJA in a tough position, because if they didn't accept our recommendation, then it would look as if they'd be going against their rider's wishes; and if they gave in to us, then it set new precedents and demonstrated how much power we actually had if we came together. It may sound like a pretty aggressive stance on our part, but we were passionate about the system working fairly and squarely – ultimately to progress our industry – and by bringing our voices together, we were in a strong position. So it was that Derek was offered the job.

UK Sport's World Class Performance initiative had started getting involved with showjumping by this point and was providing significant lottery funding. This meant that the Chef d'Equipe job was a salaried rather than voluntary position. The powers that be in the World Class team supported the idea of the riders having a voice. Apart from anything else, it made their jobs easier because if the guy we picked didn't work out and we weren't successful, it was our own fault for picking him in the first place.

As it was, Derek was Chef d'Equipe for nine years before Rob Hoekstra took over as Performance Manager in 2010. In my opinion Derek had been the right man for the role at the time and he did a good job. He made in-roads into improving the role and communication channels greatly. But, as with all things in life, nothing lasts forever and it's most definitely a role with a shelf-life for anyone who takes it.

I also started getting involved with the marketing of the BSJA at around this time, which led to various other roles for me. I was actually enjoying being involved in the politics of the sport, gaining confidence to try to move things along. I have always felt that if you have something to say, say it – and back it up. I know some people consider me outspoken and probably wish I'd keep quiet sometimes, but I'm nothing if not honest and everything I do, I do for the good of my sport. I've been on a lot of committees – the BSJA, Olympia International Horse Show, the European Championships, the Olympic Games Legacy Committee – so I guess my opinions have got me noticed over the years. But as long as the outcome has been positive and has helped the sport to evolve, then I'm happy. I want the sport to improve, develop and go forward.

Not only was the political dynamic of the sport changing, so too were the technicalities. Showjumping courses were changing and had been for the last few years. Poles were lighter, tracks were more complicated and you needed a different type of horse to do well. Bridget was a good, old-fashioned type of horse and the new courses just didn't suit her. Percy, on the other hand, found the new style relatively easy and he was going well at the UK shows, but Bridget was struggling when we went abroad. I decided to switch their roles and started taking Parcival (Percy) to the big shows on the Continent as my Grand Prix horse. And it paid off…

The first show we went to was in Switzerland and I ended up being Leading Rider of the show, partly due to Woody being placed in every class he went in and Percy finishing third in the Grand Prix. At that point, I knew he was ready for the big time. Kevin and Jeanette Edwards of Traxdata were still my sponsors and Bridget was their horse, whereas the Garratts owned Parcival. I was well aware that if Percy was to become my main horse, I'd need to have a conversation with Kevin and Jeanette.

While I was anxious about the call, I was hoping the Edwards would be understanding and they were. All they were concerned with was me fielding the best team possible and winning the most classes, as this would reflect well on their brand. Bridget would still be going to the big shows, she just wouldn't be jumping in all the big classes. Funnily enough, though, Bridget became more of a star after this, as we concentrated on specialist classes – puissances, the Derby, the classes that attract the most viewing public because of the thrills and spills. She actually became a better horse, because these classes suited her down to the ground and she won more money, even though she was doing less.

Meanwhile, Ann and Colin Garratt bought me a second horse in 2001 – his name was Landed Gentry, or Archie in the stable. I had a horse for every class and they were all, without question, the bee's knees. I had the whole package. However, just when I thought things couldn't get any better, along came another exciting prospect in the form of a giant four-year-old grey mare called Ruby (Corlato).

John Bosher had acquired her as a foal and brought her over for me to break in. I hadn't been too sure about her at first, because she just had too much brute strength. But when we jumped her under saddle for the first time, I couldn't help but feel excited. She was incredible, so I told John to take her home and give her the summer off, then I'd have her back to work on the following winter. Things were going well and I was being invited to Aachen, Calgary, Dublin – all the top shows. And then I had a phone call out of the blue – did I want to be involved in a Channel 4 series called 'Faking It'?

Chapter 22

Faking It

- ● Roped in
- ● Shelley, the podium dancer
- ● Celebrity success
- ● A sneaky cover-up

Our sport doesn't receive half the television coverage it used to back in its heyday, so when a programme featuring anything remotely equestrian hits our screens, the whole horsey community starts talking about it. This was the case with 'Faking It'. So when I was given the opportunity to be involved in the making of one of the episodes, I didn't hesitate, in spite of my initial reticence with 'Cutting Edge' a few years earlier. Besides, this sounded like fun and a real challenge.

Although I was approached in March of 2001 by Channel 4 on an advisory basis, I was eventually roped in as the on-camera trainer. The concept of the series was that a chosen person had one month to learn a new trade, then at the end of that time they'd take an oral and practical test, set by industry experts, to test their skills in a 'final' on the last day. So for our 'fake', that meant answering a series of questions about horses and showjumping from a set of predetermined questions and jumping around a course of 1.10m in a show environment. There would be three other people, all experienced in the profession, performing and taking the test on the same day. The judges would have to try and pick out the faker. Some of the other episodes were 'Sheepshearer to Hairdresser', 'Ballet Dancer to Wrestler' and ours was 'Showgirl to Showjumper'.

When I agreed to be the trainer, I told the production company I'd need someone to help me as I had never taught a beginner in my life. So I asked Mary-Anne Trevor-Roper to lend a hand and she was fantastic. She is the most organised, disciplined person I have ever met – a real diamond. She helped me find all the horses and plan out the schedule. Even though I was confident that we'd be able to get the person up to speed in time, there were certain criteria we'd need to fulfil to ensure we had the right 'faker' for the job. They needed to be fit and agile, and they needed to be tough and not worried about falling off – because that goes with the territory and probably would happen. So the production company agreed, and after much frantic preparation, Shelley Elvin arrived.

One of the rules of the programme was that we weren't allowed to meet our pupil until the first day of filming, so I knew nothing about Shelley until she pulled up in my yard and got out of the cab in her Lycra and high heels. The show's directors wanted our reactions when we met for the first time to be natural and authentic. I'm pretty sure they got what they wanted from me – my face was a picture. Shelley was a podium dancer from London, she was very bubbly and had come from a difficult background. She was one of life's colourful characters – with ripe language to match.

Shelley was very clear from the beginning that she was using the show as a stepping stone to fame and fortune. And she'd tell us how she had it all planned out in her mind – when she was accepting her Oscar for Best Actress, she would thank everyone and say that it had all begun with 'Faking It'. Although she loved animals, it turned out that she was really scared of the bigger ones and I noticed on the first day that right from the start, she would jump and twitch if one of the horses moved suddenly.

Strangely, Shelley hadn't really grasped when she started the programme that if she didn't complete the task and learn to ride properly, her failure would be broadcast on national TV. I think she thought that if she wasn't up to scratch by the end, then a body double would stand in to take her place in the final. When reality hit home and she realised that the final outcome and success hinged on her and her alone, she panicked and went into meltdown. So we had to pick her up psychologically and keep pushing her onward after the first few days.

To help Shelley hit the ground running, Mary-Anne and I decided to get Shelley working from walk to canter straight off, as that would be quicker, so we brought in a vaulting horse for the first week. That way, we could concentrate on her position without her having to worry about what the horse was doing. Then we were loaned two schoolmasters from a riding school to teach her to jump for the second and third weeks; a horse for the final – Bobby – who she'd be able to jump a course of 1.10m on; plus a couple of spares for practice. There was a lot to do.

Bobby turned out to be a saint. He was in his late teens and an ex-eventer, but we didn't want him to work Shelley out. We were hoping that if we trained her well enough, she could even fake it to Bobby as well as the judges. There was no way that one horse would have stood taking orders from a beginner for long – they suss out new riders quickly and often take advantage by not doing as they're told, no matter how sweet-natured they are.

Anyway, we realised that Shelley needed to be walking and cantering within five days of first sitting on a horse, jumping by the end of the first week, jumping down a grid by the second week and jumping courses by the third. On top of this, she had to learn the theory that goes with horse care in order to pass the oral part of the final exam – points of the horse, basic ailments, the showjumping competition structure, things like that. One thing was for sure, though – there was a lot of money going into this production and I felt under pressure to get this girl up to speed by the set targets. There was no pussy-footing around.

Shelley had to live and breathe the whole horsey lifestyle. So not only was she on this punishing schedule, she had to sleep in a room in my staff accommodation that was decorated from top to bottom in horse merchandise. Bed cover, pillowcases, artwork, posters – the production company had left no stone unturned and covered her room with horsey paraphernalia. What's more, she wasn't allowed near a phone and all her letters were screened before she sent them. While cutting her off from the outside world seemed tough, more worrying was the actual discomfort she was suffering from riding.

Shelley was used to wearing high heels, but because she had to keep her heels down when riding, she started to complain about her Achilles tendon, saying that it was agony. In fact, it got so bad that I asked my horse physiotherapist, Anna Johnson, to have a look at Shelley, reassure her that this was probably nothing more than different muscles working in a way they weren't used to and help put her mind at ease. But Anna took one look at Shelley and confirmed that she had strained her Achilles – and if this was a normal situation she would tell her not to ride for a month. So we had to strap the poor girl's legs each time she rode to try to alleviate the pain, but there was no let-up in the schedule.

As much as Shelley was a lovely girl, she didn't do herself any favours in some respects. For the final, the production company had set aside a small budget for some gear so she could look the part, but it was a measly amount so I said to them: "If you want her to look like one of us, you need to get her some decent gear."

So we took her out and spent about £800 on breeches, a jacket, hat, leather boots and a shirt for her – really lovely stuff. She looked fabulous in it all, but came out of the changing room and announced: "I look skank." I couldn't believe what I was hearing. Most riders would have given their eye teeth to be kitted out in such quality gear.

While I was really annoyed at her for this ungrateful attitude, Shelley was a hard worker and a good pupil – at least, when she was on the horse. But she would never be up in time to muck out or feed her horse in the morning. The staff would complain that she kept them up with her music until 3am every night, so it was no wonder she couldn't get up. She had a camera to record a video diary while we were making the show. I wasn't allowed to see it during filming, but afterwards I saw a few clips, mostly of

Shelley complaining about having to get out of bed. Never once did she consider that her horses might need to eat and be cared for – the main concern was her own beauty sleep.

All in all, we did have some fun with her that month, after filming was done and before the programme was aired in November. She became quite a little celebrity in the horse world and was invited to the 'Horse & Hound' ball and the BSJA ball. To be fair to Shelley, she came so close to pulling it off in the final. She rode beautifully, but the questions in the oral round let her down. The judges for the final were Peter Robeson, Graham Fletcher and Derek Ricketts. They had a list of 20 questions from which they were allowed to pick five to ask her. Shelley had been drilled and drilled on these questions, evening after evening, but when Derek Ricketts asked her what she was aiming for that year, she answered that she would love to qualify for the 'Foxhunters' final. As soon as she said 'Foxhunters plural', I knew we were sunk – it's Foxhunter singular. Mary-Anne tried to reassure me that they hadn't noticed. Derek asked again: "So you want to qualify for the Foxhunters? Is that right?"

"Yeah, the Foxhunters," She replied. One small slip and she was spotted as the fake. It was a real shame, she'd done brilliantly up to then.

When it came to saying goodbye, it was quite emotional and I was sad to see her go as she was such a character. However, the one thing that really disappointed me was that Shelley didn't go to see her horse before she left. Once she'd jumped off Bobby the day of the final, it was as if he no longer existed – his job was done and she felt no attachment to him or gratitude for his fine work. I was really disappointed in her for that. And as she left, I said to Laura: "You know, she never mucked out once while she was here."

There was quite a lot of controversy surrounding the programme when they started airing in the autumn, so the team at Channel 4 told us we could have a screening of it in their London headquarters before it went out. As I was watching the programme, I saw footage of Shelley mucking out.

"That didn't happen," I told the producer. I was confused as

I knew she had never mucked out a single horse during her stay with me.

"I forgot to tell you," Laura piped up. "While you were jumping in Modena, the crew called me and asked if they could come back and film a bit more footage."

It turned out that the storyline they were trying to sell involved Shelley bucking her ideas up after a good talking to from me, and her then getting up and mucking out the next morning. What she had actually done was ignored me and carried on sleeping in, so the production team had brought her up to the yard for an hour while I was away to film her mucking out a horse and jumping up and down on my muck heap for good measure. But if you look closely at the footage of Shelley mucking out, you can see that her hair is a different colour than during the rest of the show – and she's wearing a baseball cap.

The crew had pitched up to find she had dyed her hair red since filming had finished and they'd had to run off to the local chemist's to try to find a dye that would change it back to her natural light brown colour. Unable to achieve the desired effect, she'd been made to cover up with a baseball cap but tufts of red were clearly escaping from beneath it for all to see. We kept in touch for a while and she kept up riding. 'Faking It' was tough but it did my reputation as a trainer no harm!

Chapter 23

Life is a rollercoaster

- BSJA training scheme
- Fresh Direct
- Revisiting Ruby
- A father again

Besides 'Faking It', it was a busy year for me away from the competitions. I was getting more and more involved with elections, committees and policies in the BSJA. There were now more regular opportunities to give something back to my sport, which I have always been keen to do. One of the most ambitious of those opportunities was involvement with the BSJA Accredited Coaches pyramid.

I had been approached by John Lanni, chairman of the BSJA training committee, to be part of a new scheme – an accredited coaching programme – being pioneered by the BSJA. Teaching and training in equestrian sports can sometimes be pretty ad hoc, so I thought it great that our governing body wanted to improve the general standards of riding in British showjumping. Particularly encouraging was the focus on younger up-and-coming riders who represented the sport's future.

There are a lot of 'teachers' out there in the industry who've never taken any form of professional qualification. Yet they make the majority of their money from training, as did I, over many years. Just because someone has been successful in a sport doesn't mean they should teach or can teach. The BSJA wanted to educate and unify training practices – get everyone singing from the same hymn sheet. To me, that made a lot of sense. I was very excited about the scheme.

Initially, about 12 of us from all around the country were recruited. We were hand-picked by John Lanni to work with Swedish trainer, Lars Sederholm, Head BSJA Coach – the man at the top of the 'pyramid', as they called it. Lars would produce a master training manual on which we would all base our teaching. This blueprint would be the basis for all future training at the top of the sport by accredited coaches. It would then filter down, step by step, to the lower levels, right down to the grass roots. That, anyway, was the grand idea. It was an ambitious plan and by no means a small undertaking. This bold initiative had the potential to revolutionise the sport, and to improve teaching and riding standards at every level.

The format was to involve Lars going to each of the trainers' yards and taking each of us for one full day of private training per month over a three-year period. It would be interspersed by regular group training sessions with other 'chosen ones' from our respective areas. Those trainers most local to me were Di Lampard, Andy Austin, Tony Newbery and Johnny Harris. Now, I have a lot of respect for Lars as a trainer but I found him to be quite a domineering teacher. Lars had his own, prescribed way of doing things, even down to dictating precise phrases he wanted you to use as a coach. Seemingly, there was no discussion or variation allowed.

John Lanni had put his heart and soul into the scheme – Lars too – and they obviously wanted it to succeed. I did as well but Lars' intensity, coupled with me being a bit stressed and overworked, meant that about halfway through the three-year training period, things came to a head. It was at a group training session and Lars was watching me teach a young rider. We were doing some lateral work but Lars wasn't happy with my phrasing so he stopped me. I told him that the pupil understood me perfectly, even though I was using different words to his. He didn't agree and demanded I use his exact phrasing.

Neither of us would back down, so I ended up completing the course out of class.

It's a shame that the scheme fell short of its potential. Lars ended up leaving his post as Head Coach earlier than planned. I don't think the process had been what he had envisaged when he agreed to be part of it, although most of the trainers completed the course under his tuition before he left. Lars was succeeded at the BSJA by Di Lampard who finished off my training. If I'm honest, though, I'd been so busy with a yard full of horses that I hadn't given it my undivided attention at the time. I'd also been consumed in looking for a new sponsor.

Things with Kevin and Jeanette Edwards were about to come to an end. Traxdata's fortunes had changed and they had to pull out of showjumping. We'd had a fabulous time – they'd been so generous and supportive, not just to me, but to showjumping in general. Wiston Bridget was still kept with me and she was part of the team of horses, along with Parcival, Landed Gentry and Glenwood Springs. I had a horse for every course, so I knew that if I kept up the good results and my ear to the ground, something would come up.

One generous, ingenious idea for Olympia that year came from David Ashby of Amlin Plus Insurance. David asked if there was any way of sponsoring me for just the one show. After some discussion, the BSJA gave me special dispensation to carry the Amlin logo for the week. The deal worked really well for David, who had clients at the show, by adding value to the brand. There are always opportunities around the corner – you just have to look for them. David has remained a sponsor and supporter ever since.

With Parcival, Landed Gentry and Glenwood Springs, I was getting some great results and then we were hit by another minor blow. Bridget was being used for more selective classes but I'd decided to take her to Modena, Italy where she tested positive for a derivative of a banned substance. The amount was so minute that it seemed obvious she had picked it up from left-over feed in one of the show's permanent boxes. The show stables were a riding club and school the rest of the year, so a huge number of horses would be coming and going. They would be mucked out for the show, but the stables still contained old bedding and leftover feed, so we should have been more careful. But we weren't and we paid the price.

There are rules in place now that ensure stabling is sterilised before being used for an international show and it's cases like mine, where a horse has accidently picked something up, that brought them into play. The FEI accepted this was accidental and gave me a small fine and no ban. I did have to put in an appeal to the British Olympic Association prior to the Olympics to allow me to be selected but that was just a formality.

After all the trouble of proving our innocence, a trip to Cannes to pick us up seemed too good an offer to miss. Wow! What a great place for a show – just along the beach front, two minutes' walk from the famous film festival. I thought Woody and Percy would like the movie star lifestyle and they did. John Bosher came along for the weekend with a friend of his, Les Harris. I won two classes, so on the Saturday evening, we had a glass of champagne to celebrate and I got talking to Les about his son, Colin, who had been a very promising Young Rider. He had stopped riding to help with the running of Les's business, Fresh Direct. As the name suggests, it's a company that supplies top-quality fresh fruit and veg to restaurants, hotels, luxury stores, events companies and also to many of the caterers at top shows. Les had always maintained his interest in horses and showjumping.

At the end of the evening Les announced: "I think I should sponsor you."

"I was thinking exactly the same thing." I replied. "I'll do you a special deal. You can sponsor me for six months including the rugs, jackets, lorry and horse names. It will include Olympia."

"Done." he said, completing the deal with a proper handshake. Since then, Fresh Direct has increased its annual turnover from £11 million to £150 million. Long may it continue!

My first big show in Fresh Direct colours was the Hickstead Derby, where I was favourite to win with Bridget after her double clear two years earlier. Geoff Billington always said of the

We've always had cats and dogs around the yard, and Inga lived to the ripe old age of 20

Border collie Tip follows me around everywhere and Corgi-cross Spice is just out to play with anyone

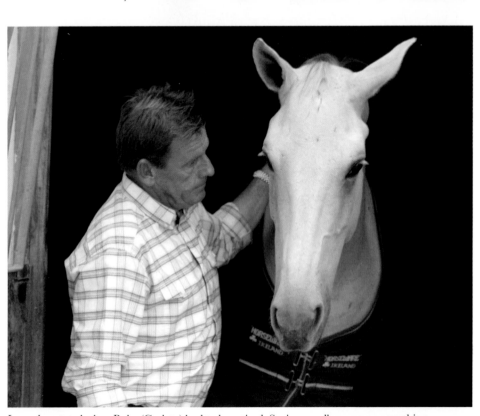

I was devastated when Ruby (Corlato) had to be retired. Saying goodbye was no easy thing

Skiing is a sport we all enjoy but Laura's the real speed merchant

This was the one I wanted to win – the King George V Gold Cup, on Fresh Direct Kalico Bay

Little and large. Me, Joseph and Beauty posing for British Showjumping

Three men in a boat. Taking time out from a competition in Calgary

Joseph takes his jumping very seriously (here on Twilight Blue) and is a keen Pony Club member

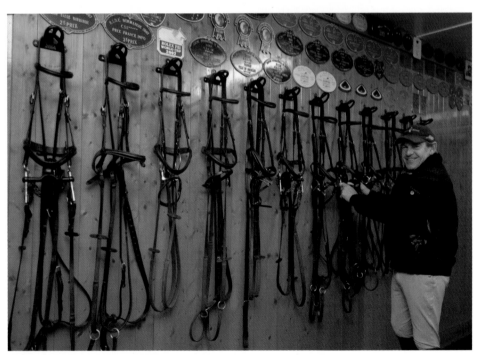

I like everything to be neat and tidy – a trait picked up from Graham Fletcher

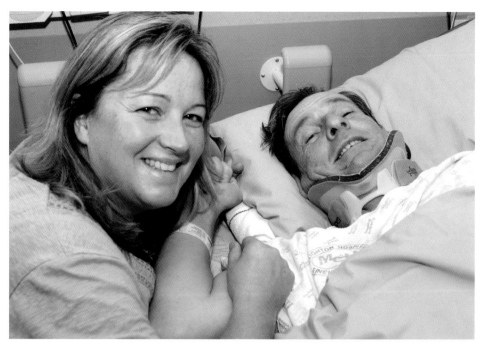

Lying on my back for six weeks was not a barrel of laughs, but visits from Laura kept my spirits up

My killer collar. It made me itchy and hot, and I couldn't wait to get rid of it

Dovecote Farm would grind to
a halt if it wasn't for Laura

Horses are a way
of life, a vocation,
so when I'm not
competing, there's
always other business
to take care of

Mark (above) having fun on Beauty at
Addington Manor. Whether Joseph or
Mark follow in my footsteps remains to be
seen. If not, there's always cricket!

course's outstanding feature: "To other horses it was a bank, to Bridget it was a speed bump!" But this time, when I got to the top of that famous Derby Bank, Bridget just walked straight off the top and out into thin air. We'd been clear till then.

As ever, I was powerless to stop her. Needless to say, she landed at the bottom almost face first and catapulted me into the ground. I got up feeling groggy but otherwise okay, but Bridget was a bit unlevel. We later found out that this stunt had torn a ligament in her foot. After resting her for a few months, we tried a couple of times to bring her back into work, hoping that the injury had healed. Sadly, though, she would go lame again. Bridget's career was at an end.

We still had the World Equestrian Games in Jerez, Spain, coming up that summer and I should have known better than to go and try horses in Belgium. I was trying a young horse which tipped up with me, breaking my collarbone. The dealer took me to a Belgian hospital where they wanted to plate it, but I wasn't having that. I discharged myself and got a taxi to the airport. On the way, I phoned David McPherson, from whom I had bought Percy.

"David," I said, "I need you to do me a favour and jump Parcival for me in Gijon next week. I need him to jump if he's to be ready for Jerez." He agreed without a moment's hesitation.

With my limp arm in a sling, all I could think about was how I was going to have the horse ready for the Championships. It never once entered my mind that I might not be ready, or that I was putting the team in jeopardy by insisting on jumping.

I thought I'd best tell Derek Ricketts about my plan to get David to ride. "Derek, I've broken my collarbone," I explained, "but I'm going to be fine for Jerez. David is jumping Parcival next week in Gijon so the horse will be ready. I just need to take it easy, but I'll be fine."

I told Derek what was going to happen despite the fact that it was down to him and not me and I still think he was so shocked by my idea, he just went along with it to keep me quiet. He agreed to hold the place and to allow David to jump Percy. I guess I did steamroller him into it, but this was my first chance in the big leagues and I wasn't going to let that go. David did a great job of preparing the horse; and my doctor did a great job of patching me up. With a bottle of painkillers glued to my good hand, I flew off to Spain full of anticipation.

I did make it to Jerez, but the team didn't do that well. It was a great experience for me, though, and I got a real taste for the major championship occasion. As a team, we put in a pretty mediocre performance, finishing 16th, but I was pleased with Parcival – we'd done well together finishing 35th overall and I was the highest placed Brit.

When Ann and Colin came to me and asked me to buy a horse, all they wanted was one capable of having a chance of getting in to the Foxhunter Final. Ann had finally got a passport and enjoyed travelling to shows abroad but they both still loved Horse of the Year Show. The trip to Jerez had been amazing but there was still more to come that would surpass all expectations.

When Percy was placed on the first day at Horse of the Year Show, they were thrilled. Then when he won the Grand Prix, it was so fantastic, words can't describe their elation. It is a special class to win and one that all owners and riders enjoy, but for Ann and Colin it was more than a dream come true. Ann spoke to me the next morning from her kitchen, where she said she was sitting staring at the trophy with a silly grin on her face saying to herself, "PERCY WON THE GRAND PRIX, PERCY WON THE GRAND PRIX!" Riders often focus on the prize money but it wasn't about that for Ann and Colin. They just love showjumping and winning a title at Horse of the Year Show was priceless.

There are massive highs and massive lows in all sport, especially where animals are concerned. Riders have to learn to bounce back from problems losing horses to injury or having to retire them due to age. I hate having to make decisions to retire horses – it's a horrible time. They've been your friend and team mate and you've got to know them and their quirks and traits. There are so many showjumping riders who have had to really pick themselves up after the loss of a horse, I don't think I could even start to list them. What I do know, though, is that we must all have in us the same gene somewhere that drives us on to search out another one and produce it into a Grand Prix horse. I just wish all our horses could finish on a high. I might sound romantic but they deserve it.

And so the rollercoaster dips again, leaving me low on horses. Bridget was officially retired to stud duties, while Landed Gentry sustained a tendon injury and had six months off as a result. Retiring with a stifle injury, Percy went home to Ann and Colin and has a very cosy life as a pet. On the upside, I still had a very nice bunch of novice horses, including Brisante, Pircolando M and Roland. And for the bigger classes, there was my good old faithful, Glenwood Springs, now joined by short-term rides – Jerome and Cloudy Night, owned by John Nichol at Headley Stud near Newbury, Berkshire.

It was about this time that the big grey mare, Corlato (Ruby), returned to my yard. I'd sent her back to her owner, John Bosher, after trying her as a four-year-old, thinking that she would have a rest over the summer before coming back in the winter. I had phoned John up after the summer and asked him when he wanted me to have the mare back, as I was keen to see if she was as good as I thought she might be. He told me that Ruby had not, in fact, enjoyed a summer off. She'd been working – jumping and going to shows.

I went to see her at John's place and was really disappointed with what I found. She'd lost all her lovely shape over a fence and she was running at the jumps with her head up – so I told him I didn't want the horse back. He could keep her, as I felt she'd been messed up. The following year John asked me to come and have another look. Ruby felt so strong and powerful, despite the bad habits she had picked up, and she had so much jump that I thought it would be stupid to turn her down. So as a rising six-year-old – a year later than planned – I got Corlato back.

The next 12 months were spent consolidating and planning the careers of my next set of horses, with national shows and Young Horse classes. But the undoubted highlight later that year came when Laura announced she was pregnant again. I was so excited about the fact that we were having another beautiful baby… and then, just to bring me back down to earth, I had another crashing fall.

Chapter 24

Taking the knocks

- Cloudy to clear
- A fast delivery
- Bravery pills
- A stitch-up

Runs of good and bad luck have one thing in common: they don't last forever. I was sure I'd had the worst of it by the spring of 2004 and things would start looking up. Landed Gentry came back well from his injury to become one of my best horses, so I took him, Woody and my new ride, Cloudy Night, to Nantes, France. Cloudy was a funny mare, she was narcoleptic and would fall asleep at the drop of a hat. She had the same breeding as the famous giant grey horse, Calvaro, ridden by Willi Melliger.

It's very rare to find mature horses with this problem because they usually break their limbs or necks, dropping to the ground and rarely surviving. Cloudy would be in the stable at home and you could hear the smack as she hit the floor and then she'd get up again as if nothing had happened. We had to make sure she always had a deep bed, always wore bandages and had no weave bar to get tangled up on. Thankfully, she never dropped off while being ridden – the vet said it had something to do with the adrenaline rush during exercise.

Cloudy Night was a good mare with a big jump but she always kept me on my toes. We were jumping in Nantes, France.

The show had gone okay for me and I'd won a few quid during the week, but I wasn't optimistic about Cloudy's chances in the Grand Prix. I went to the organisers to explain that I needed to go early in the class in order to catch a flight. Usually riders prefer to go later in the draw, so they agreed and put me fourth to go. I warmed up as usual, went in and the horse jumped a lovely clear. Flaming typical!

There were 50-odd entries in the class, so now I had to wait ages for the jump-off, likely to have a good dozen people in it. I sat and watched the other riders go one by one, and with just five to go, there were still no clear rounds. I couldn't believe it. By now, I'd missed my flight, but could win some good prize money here. By the end of the first round, it was just me and Hauke Luther on Caresino who'd gone clear. Ever the opportunist, I went up to Hauke and asked him if he wanted to pool and split first and second prize.

I knew I was on the lesser horse, so if I could persuade him to pool the money, it might mean an extra few grand. We would still go in and jump off for the crowd, but it would already be settled behind the scenes. I have often seen a class really come alive in the jump-off after the riders have agreed to split the prize money before they go in. It means they've nothing to lose so throw caution to the wind. Anyway, Hauke wanted to see it out. He knew he was on the better horse and was confident he could beat me. I went first and Cloudy Night jumped another lovely clear round. Hauke had a fence down so I ended up winning fair and square. The win came totally out-of-the-blue which made it even more memorable. Of course, I was more than happy to buy a new plane ticket after that.

Laura's timing couldn't have been better – she went into labour just as I arrived at The British Open in Sheffield. "It's okay, my parents are coming to visit, I'll be fine," she told me. I had trouble concentrating that first night but the horses all jumped well. I raced back home and in the early hours Mark James was born. A beautiful brother for Joseph. That morning I couldn't tear myself away so I was a bit late heading back to Sheffield and the traffic was heavy. I made it to the collecting ring with about five horses to go. My groom was already warming up Woody for me. I had a quick look at the course, jumped a few fences and that was it. In we went and Woody, ever the superstar, won it for us. The papers were full of it, with the next day's headline exclaiming, 'Stockdale Delivers On Time!'.' That wasn't the best of it: Woody won again the next day, too. He must have known there was another mouth to feed.

My sponsor and Fresh Direct owner, Les, and his wife, Fay, love coming out to shows to give support. That's great, as I love having people around me when I'm jumping. It's wonderful to share success with friends and supporters. The Irish shows are always very sociable occasions and Belfast International is no exception. Les had come out to the show for the weekend and we stayed in the most bombed hotel in Europe, The Europa. Belfast's Odyssey Arena is so atmospheric and steeped in shipbuilding history. It's a rare setting, with two massive cranes dating back to the days of the Titanic.

Every night we went to the riders' party and had an absolute ball – me thinking I needed to look after my sponsor; and him thinking he needed to look after his rider, but neither of us looking after each other. I won the hotly-contested puissance on the Saturday night with a horse called Lavaletto, who I'd borrowed from Robert Smith. Les and I got no sleep on our last celebratory night in Belfast – we just went straight from the bar to the airport. Some of the best memories I have are of winning classes that aren't necessarily the most prestigious, but those I associate with good times. That weekend in Belfast with Les Harris was one of them.

I've had a few horses come to me over the years with all sorts of lotions and potions but only one has arrived with 'bravery pills'. This mare arrived when I got back from Northern Ireland. She was very hot, a blood horse, with a big jump and I was quite excited to have her on the yard. When she was dropped off, I was given a bag with about 10 triangular pills.

"What are these?" I asked the owner.

"They're bravery pills. You need to give them to her about

an hour before she jumps," he replied. I laughed and spluttered: "Seriously?"

"They readdress the balance in her brain and they make her brave," the man said.

The mare stayed with me for a while. She jumped really well and we started getting some good results. When I saw the owner a few weeks later, he remarked: "Those pills are working well, Tim, you must be getting low on them, I'll get you some more. Use them wisely, they're very expensive."

It turned out he was spending £75 for 10 of these triangle things. So the next time my vet, Thorsten, was at the yard, I asked him what they were.

"They're dog worming pills, Tim," came the reply. Thorsten did a bit of research for me and found out they cost pennies, not pounds, each. I was furious that this person was being ripped off so I decided to tell him what was going on. Obviously he was as shocked as I'd been when given the pills in the first place. I'm afraid nothing is going to make a horse brave except a good bit of riding.

There's always someone out there willing to sell you something that's going to turn your horse into a superstar. Don't get me wrong, I believe it's important to get proper advice and we have our vet in nearly every week checking things. He consults regularly with our farrier, Nigel, and physiotherapist, Anna. We also have regular discussions with an equine nutritionist.

Call me old-fashioned but I'm not a great believer in all that other clap-trap. There are alternative therapists who, if they were working on humans, wouldn't get past 'go', as we would know whether or not the treatment was effective. Obviously our horses can't tell us that, so these 'therapists' get away with all their mumbo jumbo.

I was once asked if a well-known 'horse whisperer' could come to my yard to assess my horses' 'souls'. I forget why – I think it was for a magazine article. She tried to tell me that one of them had been a war horse in Flanders and that 'he' had been injured in the war in a past life. I then pointed out to her that the horse was, in fact, a mare. I don't think she appreciated my input. Funny that: she could see into the past but not beyond the end of her nose.

Perhaps Brisante needed a horse whisperer to remind her to pick up her feet the day she tipped me up at home. I was doing a combination uphill in my jumping paddock. It was about 1.45m – vertical, one stride to an oxer, two strides and out over a vertical. She hit the back rail of the middle oxer on her way down and flipped straight over. I was initially thrown clear of her before she crashed to the ground but, as she got up, she kicked my head and stood on my left hand. I was unconscious for a good while and my tongue was lodged in the back of my throat, stopping me from breathing. Luckily, my groom was able to clear my airway and put me into the recovery position. Apparently, by the time the ambulance arrived, I'd got up and was walking.

I'd suffered a minor bleed on my brain, which caused memory loss for a few hours and had also shattered my left thumb. Other than that, I was in one piece. When the surgeon came to see me about my hand, he told me that, after he'd reconstructed the digit and fixed it in place with steel rods, it might not be as mobile as it had been. I told him that was probably going to be an issue as I already had a claw hand. If it got any worse, I wouldn't be able to hold the reins at all. Another doctor came and inspected the fibrous lump that had built up from the abscess I'd had 25 years before.

"My God. What is that? Do you have shortening of the tendons in your hand?" he asked.

"No, I stitched up my own hand when I was a lad and it got infected. This is what's left," I explained.

"I'll have a look in there when I open you up and see what I can do," he said.

The doctor put two pins in my thumb to hold it in place and dug out the mass of scar tissue around the joint. There was quite a long healing period and during that time, I had to ride with looped reins, as I couldn't grip normal ones. Still, my hand didn't hamper me too much – as long as I remembered the pins and didn't poke my eye wiping the sweat from my brow.

We were excited about Ruby's first Nations Cup in Lisbon. She had been going really well and I felt she was ready. The course was firm but fair and the mare was jumping really well as we turned towards the water jump. I met it just right, but as she took off over the small white board, I knew I was in trouble. She jumped it like it was a canter pole on the floor at home, landing right in the middle of the water jump. It was deep water so it tripped her up and we came crashing to the ground. Ruby's shoulder rammed straight into the concrete pool, while I was jettisoned 20ft forward, coming to rest in an unconscious heap on the floor.

I don't remember what happened next because I was out cold, but David McPherson later explained. Apparently they'd helped Ruby out of the water jump, hopping lame and bleeding heavily from her shoulder, which turned out to be fractured we later found out. I was a bit groggy and in pain, but told everyone I'd be fine after a sit-down. I was adamant that I didn't want to go to hospital even though I couldn't breathe. David McPherson took me back to my hotel for a lie-down after I insisted I was fine and just bruised. I'm terrible when injured. I don't listen to well-meant or professional advice and try to carry on regardless.

I woke up in the middle of the night in Portugal, sweating and panicking – I thought I was dying. The pain was unreal and I was struggling for breath, wheezing like an asthmatic. I couldn't move or get to the phone. It took me an hour to put on some trousers and get a jumper around my neck which I couldn't pull down. Then I phoned Michael Mac, who was standing in as Chef d'Equipe, to help me dress and get downstairs. He tried desperately to convince me to go to a hospital, but I was having none of it.

I flew home that morning and the next day started work as Head Coach on Sport Relief's 'Only Fools on Horses' TV production. I was coughing up blood during the first day of the show, so the production doctors took me off to hospital to be X-rayed, only to find I had 10 ribcage fractures and my side was black with bruises. If anyone touched me, I thought I'd faint with pain. The good news was that none of my ribs were out of line and the fractures were mostly hairline ones. I just had to wait for them to heal. There was nothing the doctors could really do for me other than prescribe heavy-duty painkillers which I scoffed like sweets. So, with me as Head Coach in a slightly druggy haze, 'Only Fools on Horses' got under way.

Chapter 25

Only Fools on Horses

- Reality TV
- Tears and tantrums
- The fall guys
- The last laugh

Looking back now, 'Only Fools on Horses' was one hell of a project and we only got away with it by the skin of our teeth. When you mix horses, amateur riders, celebrities and the demands of TV, you could be asking for trouble. That said, however, I'm always up for a challenge. Admittedly there were times when I wondered why on earth I'd got involved. But if I'm honest, I wouldn't have missed the opportunity for anything. Although it was very hard work, the benefits have far outweighed the long hours, the moans, the tears, the falls and the upsets.

Personally, I feel the show was a triumph and put showjumping back on the map. It brought together a fantastic bunch of people, all willing to put their necks on the line for Sport Relief. From the word go, the risks of the job were explained to the celebs, which they all accepted. Each and every one of them put their heart and soul into making the show the success it was. We had Jenni Falconer, Nicki Chapman (the replacement for Duncan Bannatyne, who dropped out due to injury), Matt Baker, Sara Cox, Diarmuid Gavin, Anna Ryder-Richardson,

Suzi Perry, Paul Nicholas, Sally Gunnell, Ruby Wax, Matt Littler and Josie D'Arby, who replaced Felix Dexter. It was a really mixed bunch.

It all started with each of the celebs being sent to local riding schools to learn the basic principles of riding before the intensive training began. They were all expected to be able to walk, trot and canter. Depending on how they'd fared, I'd plot how many hours I thought they each needed to get up to scratch. The process was very carefully monitored, for their benefit as well as ours. We just couldn't contemplate any serious injuries. I was there as both Head Coach and technical consultant, so if any of the wheels fell off this well-oiled machine, the buck stopped firmly with me.

By the time intensive training began on Monday 5 June, 2006, at Waresley Park in Cambridgeshire with trainers Mary-Anne Trevor-Roper, Fred Bergendorff, Mia Korenika and Jenny Ward, some of the celebrities were moaning they were feeling the pressure. Nerves were beginning to kick in, especially when we introduced them to their horses. Then by the Wednesday, it really kicked off – big time. This was the first real day of training and total carnage. After three or four of our celebrities had hit the deck, they organised a mini group protest saying the horses were wild. This just wasn't true. They were as safe, sound and well-schooled as a horse could be for that level; and were competent at their jobs. They all had to have a record, be it in showjumping, eventing, working hunter or dressage arenas, and were chosen specifically for their excellent temperaments. We'd been so careful to pick the right horses, with me assessing and riding all of them.

I explained to them that these were proper horses trained to do the job – not half-baked riding school horses. I explained that horses can think for themselves and they're unpredictable. So, although still nervy, the celebrities eventually stopped moaning and got on with it. They were all very disciplined, turning up for the two 1½-hour daily sessions, every day for 16 days of intensive training. Then came a 10-day break while we relocated to Towerlands Equestrian Centre, where we did acclimatisation training with the horses and got everything set up to start filming for Sport Relief.

As with 'Faking It', we had a very tight schedule. All the celebrities had to be walking, trotting and cantering in five days so we didn't have time for tantrums. They just needed to get on with it which, by and large, they did. I definitely don't do tears. We did have some proper nasty falls along the way. Duncan Bannatyne broke his elbow and Felix Dexter left because he had a bad tumble. He was such a big, jovial guy and pretty full of himself, but one day the horse just cannoned him into the side of the school wall. The sheer power of the horse was too much for Felix. Matt Baker was not one to give up, though. He dislocated his shoulder in a fall, then calmly got up, walked over to a wall and knocked it back in, Rambo style.

The psychological effects of a fall were one of the most interesting things to deal with during the show. A fall is something all riders experience and, as a professional, you get used to it. Each one of our riders took a tumble during the show and most were shocked by how much it hurt. Some found it hard to get back on.

One of my favourite memories was when we had the top guys from Sport Relief visiting for the day. Because of an earlier mix-up, I mistook one BBC executive for a tramp (he'd turned up looking as if he'd just got off a bench and was carrying a plastic bag as a briefcase). These arty types are difficult to spot, you know. It was suggested by one member of the crew that it would be easier to grade the executives as cheeses – ie, smelly Gorgonzola was a top executive, Cheddar was your middle man and burger slice was of low importance.

On this particular day, we had three Gorgonzolas there to visit the training camp and I was showing them round. We got as far as the outdoor arena, which had been split into four with a lesson taking place in each section. It was a wonderful sight with all this activity going on. I felt like Willy Wonka in his chocolate factory with all the oompa loompas working away. Then it went spectacularly wrong. Duncan Bannatyne fell off and his horse bolted like Frankel through the next arena, sending Fred Bergendorff flying. Suzi Perry and Jenni Falconer were trying to regain control and their horses careered into each other. The first aid paramedic appeared around the corner on her way to sort out Duncan when she misjudged a stile she was climbing. With a heavy medical rucksack unbalancing her, she fell flat on her face. With loose horses, people on the floor, lots of yelling and running about, it was quite a sight.

One of the smelly Gorgonzolas turned to me and said, I swear without any irony: "What a wonderful job you're doing here, it's sooo exciting!"

To keep the horses on the straight and narrow, they needed to have a good trip every now and then. In the morning, therefore, the trainers would sometimes jump them around the course in the main arena. This also helped some of the more nervous riders when it came to the live shows in the evening. We did have to replace one naughty horse, though. Suzi Perry's first horse was a bit of a sod and was sent back. It would charge off down the school with its head down, then stop dead and buck, sending her flying. I thought it was just something Suzi was doing until it did the same to me. It was only four weeks after I broke my ribs and when I hit the deck, I thought I would shatter into a million pieces.

Jenni Falconer won the show. She had ridden as a child, but gave up after a nasty fall. Although she was quite inexperienced, Jenni was a fighter. Plus, she had lovely balance on a horse, so looked just right. Jenni had the physique for it, too – long legs, good posture and stayed solid in the centre of the horse. What's more, she had a positive outlook and really pushed forward to a fence which gave her horse, J-Lo, confidence. But Jenni and I had an edgy relationship at first, because I was pretty hard on her. There were tears and tantrums, but I made things clear when I said: "I don't do crying, just ask my wife."

There was no mileage in being the celebs' best buddy. I had to be hard on them for their own good. Having said that, we did have a lot of fun and there are just some things about that experience I'll never forget. I was worried about Ruby Wax at first. I thought I would have my hands full, but she always listened to the trainers and only showed her fun side when she was off the horses. One day I came into the stable yard to find G-strings hanging outside her horse, Ken's, stable. Ruby also thought he deserved a fancier name, insisting his official name was now Mr Kenneth.

I'll never forget Nicki Chapman's drive and positive attitude. She came to the show late, replacing Duncan Bannatyne, so had only four days' training before we moved to Towerlands. To lift her confidence, we put her in with the better riders in order to push her. It worked – she finished second.

And I adored Sara Cox for her honesty and enthusiasm. She'd had a tough year, but kept insisting that the experience was 'a dream come true'. She may not always have come to the fence straight, or been on the right leg, but she'd get away with it more often than not because she gave her horse such a positive ride. She was a pleasure to teach.

Paul Nicholas, too, surprised me. I had a bet before the show started that he wouldn't even turn up for the first day's training, but he proved me wrong. He would always be there for his lesson on time, even though he looked as if he was going to the gas chamber. Paul was very professional – the perfect gent – and had a fantastic sense of humour which kept everyone's spirits up. He turned out to be one of my favourites.

Naturally, they all had their different strengths and weaknesses. I have a huge amount of respect for all of the celebs because they were genuinely terrified at times but carried on bravely, with lots of encouragement from the trainers. Mind you, I don't know if any of them would ever do it again.

As well as having to look after the celebs, there were also the horses to watch out for, as they'd all been kindly lent to us by their owners. They were vetted at the onset and monitored carefully throughout. Everyone worked so hard – Fred, Jenny, Mary-Anne and Mia were phenomenal, I couldn't have done it without them. The job they did was so good, people complained that it all looked so easy for the celebs. It most certainly was not.

Even Radio 1 DJ, Scott Mills, jumped on the bandwagon, announcing that anyone could do it, so we challenged him to come and try for himself. When he arrived, I could see he was looking worried. Scott had never sat on a horse before so I put him on the lunge and let him walk around. Then I told him to hold on for a little trot. I asked the horse to canter and Scott started to wobble, then fell off, crashing down on his bum. He looked pretty shaken, but I chucked him back on before leading him over to some very small jumps. A couple were up at about 1.30m so I made the horse jog and told him I would run and let the horse go so he could jump it. He was in such a state at this point, crying and shaking, that I let him get off. But I was determined to have the last laugh...

Would I do it again? Let's just say that I enjoy a challenge and sometimes find it hard to say no when probably, I should do just that.

Chapter 26

The crest of a wave

- Beijing Olympics
- Discovering Fresh Direct Kalico Bay
- Bye, bye Ruby
- King George V Gold Cup

I've got to admit I committed a cardinal sin during Ruby's come-back: I changed her bridle during the Grand Prix in St Gallen and paid the price. She had been going better than ever since she'd come back into work after fracturing her shoulder in Lisbon. My mind was focused on us being selected for the Europeans that summer in Mannheim, Germany; and for the Beijing Olympics the following year. Ruby was looking good but I kept telling everyone to calm down because things tend to come round and bite you in the bum when you second guess yourself. Sure enough they did.

In the Rome Nations Cup a few weeks before, she had been showing signs of over-keenness, rushing between distances, so I thought I needed a bit more control and put a slightly stronger bit in her mouth. She warmed up in it really well and I was looking forward to the round ahead. It was a big course at St Gallen and I knew what I had to do. But Ruby reacted to the bit and as soon as I took a hold, she backed off the bridle. As a result, we had fences down.

Needless to say, it paid off when I went back to her usual bit and concentrated on her flatwork, rather than change the bridle. We won some really good classes in the first half of the year. It got me thinking that I could really be in with a shot of making the 2008 Olympic team if I could stay on target. If I was to be in contention, I first needed to get on the Mannheim European team and I did. It was all going to plan. Ruby was consistent and I was totally focused, so I thought I was good for a place for the actual starting four.

As it turned out, I was that fifth member in Mannheim, while Ellen, John and Michael Whitaker and David McPherson all made it onto the team. Chef d'Equipe Derek Ricketts explained that while Ruby and I were going well, the others were doing better. Looking back, he was probably right, they did come home with a team bronze. It was important that we qualified for the Olympics at Mannheim which we did. Derek had rightly gone with his best team but I wasn't part of it. I was devastated.

Getting over the disappointment of Mannheim with Grand Prix wins at Royal Windsor, Nantes, Bordeaux and the British Open followed and helped to consolidate our presence. It proved that I should be considered for the following year's Olympic team. I was on target and Ruby was fit and well. All-in-all, my Olympic preparation was going to plan.

Although Ruby qualified for the World Cup finals in the spring of 2008, I decided not to go because I was entirely focused on the Olympics. After all, they needed careful preparation. To get on the Olympic team I had a plan verging on military precision. Derek Ricketts had said that he wanted me to prove to him that I could produce my horse for a specific date.

Horses are like any other athlete; they can peak too early, too late or not at all. Derek told me to choose the day I wanted him to watch and assess the horse, so I chose the Rome Nations Cup because Ruby had always gone well there. I decided to go to Royal Windsor as a warm-up for Rome and Ruby was a bit fresh there. Nevertheless, I jumped clear and four in the Grand Prix – we'd have won without that fence, I'd had the fastest time. So all in all a reasonable performance I thought. Derek, however, rang me the next day to tell me he'd had two phone calls from people telling him that Ruby hadn't jumped well at Windsor. I couldn't believe it.

"I told them I didn't care, Tim," said Derek. "You wanted me to look at the horse in Rome, so that's what I'm going to do."

I couldn't believe two people had rung Derek to tell him my horse wasn't on form just because we had one jump down – I was livid. A lot of back biting and one-upmanship goes on in our game, people trying to score points and all that. As it was, we produced an immaculate performance in Rome for Derek with a double clear, so it was job done. Derek did the same with the other Olympic contenders, telling them to produce their horses for a 'viewing' and I thought that was a fair way to assess everyone.

By the middle of May, I was feeling pretty confident that I'd be on the team, but the waiting was unbearable. Not only that, but you're stuck in limbo with your horse. Normally, I would have been busy at shows but instead we were thinking about the climate in Hong Kong. It was going to be a serious test of fitness and stamina, if we were selected.

Even though I hadn't been picked officially for the team, it was important that Ruby was acclimatised to the potential conditions. Fitness was going to be the key. She enjoyed her swimming once we got her in the pool – it took seven of us to coax her in the first time but after that she just plunged in, nearly taking her handler with her. She's a really strong swimmer and instead of just poking her nose above the surface like a hippo, she would lift her withers right out of the water.

We also started working her in the indoor school in rugs to create a sweat. In Hong Kong, one of the warm-up arenas would be air-conditioned, but the main arena was outside so it was important that we both got used to the stifling heat. I would also have to alter my warm-up routine. Usually in Europe, I take about 30 minutes to warm up before a class, but taking that amount of time in Hong Kong would waste her energy. I'd worked it out to the last detail.

To keep her in the right frame of mind and her confidence up while we were waiting for our fate to be decided, I jumped her in national shows in the 1.40m classes, and I upped my own fitness levels with regular visits to the gym.

Once I got THE PHONE CALL I'd been waiting for from Derek, I rang everyone to tell them the great news. There was one person I had to see face to face, though – my mum. She's in a care home and has Huntington's disease. She struggles with some topics, and has good and bad days. I was there for half an hour and the conversation had gone round and round in the usual fashion – she'd had ice cream for her tea, she'd got some new slippers.

"Mum," I knelt at her feet and looked into her eyes. "I'm going to the Olympic Games." There was a pause while this sunk in.

"Oh! Can I come?" she asked in delight.

It was a lovely response and totally unexpected. I hadn't thought she'd even be able to register it.

"It's in China, a long way." She looked at me again, and I swear there was a moment of comprehension then we were back in the cycle.

"I've got new slippers you know," she said.

As I was leaving and got to the bottom of the stairs, I thought, 'Damn, I'd better tell the nursing staff that if Mum starts going on about her son going to the Olympic Games, she doesn't need her meds upping, because it's true!' So I went back and knocked on the door to tell them.

I didn't really have time to get excited about the Olympics in the run-up, as there was just too much to do and organise. It wasn't until I'd been to the doctor to have the travel jabs that things started to sink in. One of the slightly irksome things in the run-up to the Games is that there are various codes of conduct you need to follow and one of those is that you must be drug tested – a lot. So every day in the six weeks before we left for Hong Kong, we had to fill out forms outlining when and where we'd be available for testing. I'd tell them that I'd be in my house between 7pm and 6am, but there was a hotline that you could ring if your whereabouts changed.

When I was at home, Adrian – my tester – would come around

one morning a week at 5.59am, with his little case and pee pot. And he had to watch me give my sample to make sure I wasn't switching pots. It wasn't a pleasant experience but one that we all had to do; I thought I'd have a joke with Michael Whitaker when we were walking the course at Hickstead a few weeks later.

"Look, the dope testers are here. They've changed their technique, you know – they grab hold of your John Thomas now and shove it in the bottle to make sure the sample is yours," I told him

"I'm not having that!" He was horrified.

"I'm telling you. It frightened the life out of me having an old boy mess around with my todger."

I don't know how I managed to keep a straight face. The best bit was Michael got selected for the random test that day. The rules are you have six hours to produce some urine so they follow you around until you do. Off Michael went, furtively glancing over his shoulder at the guy following him around, but by the end of the day he was bursting for a pee, so he practically ran to their caravan and told them he needed to go. But before the guy had a chance to show Michael to the cubicle, he grabbed a bottle, peed into it and handed it over. Michael was furious when he found out I'd been taking the pee.

Sadly his Olympic prospect, Portofino, pulled up lame in the warm-up class at the Olympics. This meant that reserve Nick Skelton and his grey stallion, Russel, were on the team. We were plagued with problems. John's horse Peppermill, was stiff with a muscular problem and was unfit for the first round of the Nations Cup. We were told he could jump the following day but under Olympic rules, because he hadn't jumped in the earlier round, he was not allowed to carry on in the competition. It was a severe blow.

The rest of us did the best we could, Ben jumped 0/4. I jumped 4/8 and Nick was on 8/13 faults, so we dropped out of the team medals and finished seventh, later to be promoted to fifth place after several horses on other teams tested positive for banned substances. I firmly believe if Peppermill had been allowed to jump, we would have won a medal.

In the individual competition, both Ben and I jumped clear, it was the most amazing feeling. Wow, the final at the Olympic Games. There were only 10 combinations of horse and rider who had a chance of winning a gold medal and I was one of them. Sadly, it didn't go to plan in the second round – for whatever reason Ruby was very tense and we had four down. Each day she'd jumped one round and been put away for the night. On that final day, we jumped then had an hour's break where she went back to her stable. I think she thought she'd finished and had switched off. When we warmed up again, she hit a fence hard and it unsettled her. I knew her well and I could tell it had had an effect on her. At the time, I was gutted but after thinking about it I was pleased with how she'd coped.

Coming back from Hong Kong was a bit of a reality shock. So it was back to the 'day job', focusing on the horses that had had to take a back seat for a few months. One of those was a lovely new horse called Kalico Bay (Frankie). I knew Frankie was special, so wanted to make sure his education was just right.

He'd come to me the year before as a six-year-old, from an Irish lady called Melanie Davidson. She came for a few days' training and brought Kalico Bay with her. She'd been having a few problems with him sticking his nose up in the air like a giraffe. He couldn't even see where he was going. She'd been riding him in draw-reins to help get his head down and sure enough, once I'd seen her ride and asked her to take them off, the cheeky beggar stuck his nose right up in the air again.

I had a sit on him, but he just stood in the corner, stamped his feet and wouldn't budge. He seemed very reluctant about everything, so a bit of gentle coaxing was required. After a few days, however, we had a jump and he suddenly came alive. He kept his frame and rhythm and jumped beautifully for me. Then Melanie had a go and again he showed an incredible agility over a fence.

"Did he jump like that for me?" I asked her groom.

"No," she said. I was disappointed. "He jumped a lot better for you."

"Really?"

"Yes, he was unbelievable."

Frankie continued to improve for the rest of his stay with us until he went home with Melanie, a completely different horse – or so I thought. It only took 24 hours for the little so-and-so to demonstrate his quirky temperament again and I was disappointed for her that the wheels had fallen off so soon.

"Can I send him over to you again, Tim," asked Melanie, "only this time for about a couple of months, so that you can work him more consistently?"

So Frankie came back to Dovecote Farm and eventually, Melanie decided that Frankie wasn't right for her. He suited me, and Ann and Colin Garratt were looking for another horse so I gave them a call.

"I've found your next horse."

"Okay, whatever you think, Tim, we'll go with it."

I was quite excited about taking him to his first show. Colin came along to watch, it was only a 1.15m class. Frankie stopped at the second fence and had two jumps down; what on earth had I done?

"It's okay, I know you know what you're doing," Colin said confidently. I hoped he was right.

I was really looking forward to the Europeans being held at Windsor. The setting is incredible of course, and the whole place is steeped in tradition and history. But I was also looking forward to getting Ruby back out there, even though she was being thrown in at the deep end in the run-up to the competition. She'd had three months off to have embryos transferred from her to surrogate mares and suffered with a virus that knocked her for six when she came back into work. So in the end, she really only had about six weeks' preparation for the championships.

However, Ruby being Ruby, she jumped out of her skin, ensuring our selection for the squad alongside Ben Maher, Geoff Billington, Robert Smith and Peter Charles. When the day of the first qualifying round finally arrived, I was feeling pretty optimistic. The arena looked fantastic, as ever, and the facilities were top-class. The team started off reasonably well, sitting seventh overall after the qualifier, then by the second day, after the first round of the team final, we'd risen to second. In the final round, however, we made a few too many mistakes, dropping us down to sixth place.

Disappointing as it was for us to come so close to a medal and fail, the most publicised aspect of the Europeans that year was the lack of spectators for the showjumping classes. Considering we're a horsey nation, it was sad that only a few hundred people turned up to watch the jumping at an arena that sat a few thousand, although the stands were nearly full for the dressage events. What's more, I can't really put my finger on why no one came to support us, other than to say that as a nation we hadn't had a great year, whereas the dressage team was definitely on the up.

With the London Olympics just three years away, we were in a pretty sorry state as a nation, considering we used to be top of the pile. After some mediocre performances in 2009, Derek Ricketts was replaced by Rob Hoekstra. I was sad to see Derek go as he'd done a good job for nine years. But with the Olympics just around the corner, it felt that a new man in charge could turn the team's fortunes around and deliver a medal in London.

I was thrilled to receive an invitation to Canada; I love Calgary and Spruce Meadows so I was really looking forward to the trip. It was Frankie who had been jumping some bigger stuff but it was his first time there and while I'd been worried that he'd be out of his depth, he showed his mettle by winning $25,000, so I was over the moon. Strangely, something had upset Ruby during the flight and she'd sat down and taken the skin off her backside. Although she was sore, she was sound when she arrived and passed the vet checks. She felt fine after a few days' light work, so I decided to jump her in the Welcome Stakes.

She jumped clear to the last fence but then almost as soon as she landed, she suddenly went lame and I thought she'd lost a shoe. As soon as I jumped off, I saw she was holding her leg out, so I took her boot off and watched her tendon visibly swell before my eyes. The vets brought a metal boot to support her leg under the fetlock and we trailered her back to the stables. The initial scan showed her tendons to be in a terrible state, with a hole high up and lesions further down. Each injury on its own would have been bad enough but together they were career-ending. I was distraught, as I wanted her to finish her career strongly. Besides, Ruby was one of the family, we all loved her and I was really sad to see her finish this way.

With Ruby retired, Frankie started to really come into his own. He was just a nine-year-old when Ruby was injured so it was a lot to put on his shoulders yet he always found everything so easy. But he really did me proud the next year when he won Grand Prix in Portugal and France and had gone well in Nations Cups in Falsterbo, Gijon and Lisbon. In the run-up to Hickstead, I felt he was ready to do some great things.

The year before had been pretty tense in the King George V – I had the fastest time in the jump-off but the last fence down on Ruby and I'd finished second to Peter Charles. When Frankie jumped clear, I felt he had a chance, he'd been a bit green in the first round, but I knew he was a quick horse and that he'd be careful. There were seven others in the jump-off. Robert Smith and Talan had set a blistering time. All I could think about as I came to the last fence was Ivan's phone call that morning, reminding me of last year's mistake in letting Ruby run to the last, having it down.

"You had been so close last year and messed up at the last. Don't do that again. Good luck!"

I took a pull and put in an extra stride. I was still faster through the finish, although it took a second to register. I looked up at the clock, I'd won. I punched the air but Frankie raced off like he'd been shot, making my victory punch in the air look more like I was swatting a wasp. Ivan did call me later to tell me I needed to work on my victory punch.

To have that trophy in my hands having beaten off all the opposition was a dream come true and the win of my career. It was strange, because even though I'd been a successful profes-sional rider for many years, when I sat on the stairs in my parent's house as a 12-year-old and watched Mike Saywell and Chainbridge on the TV, it was the King George V Gold Cup that I really wanted to win and I'd done it.

While 2010 was a year that went well professionally, my personal life took a hammering because it was the year I lost my brother Iain. Needless to say, his passing hit the family hard.

The London Olympics had been in the back of my mind, but now they were very much at the forefront. The confidence I got from winning the King George spurred me on to aim almost exclusively for London. A home Games is a once-in-a-lifetime thing and the prospect of having a horse who might be ready for it was exciting to say the least. I sat down and plotted my course through the next two years in order for me and Frankie to be in the best position to be picked for the team.

My string now consisted of a few top horses, so I started going out and looking at novices to find my next star of the future. You have to look anywhere and everywhere if you want to find a diamond in the rough, and these are the horses I tend to go for, as anything that has shown too much form at an early age tends to have a massive price tag. So my quest for a hidden gem takes me all over Europe and the UK. You often hear of a good horse at a reasonable price through word of mouth – which is how I ended up at a small yard on the side of a mountain in rainy Wales on Monday 17 October, 2011.

I'd heard that there was a talented young horse for sale there, but that he was a bit sharp – even so, he would probably be worth a look. On the way up there, I remember wondering what on earth I was doing here. The track up to the yard was a long, twisty climb full of potholes and debris, and when I arrived at the yard, the place looked tired. Nevertheless, I picked out a couple of youngsters I liked the look of, including the one I'd been told about. They brought the horses into the arena for me to try and I thought I might as well ride the one I had come here to see first then if he wasn't right, I could try the other one. So the guy legged me up…

Chapter 27

The end of the road?

- Will I walk again?
- Rock bottom
- A mental battle
- The model patient?

Even though I knew I was in a pretty bad way, all I could think of after arriving at Shrewsbury Hospital was the Olympics. "You know I've got the Olympics to go to next year, so sharpen your pencil," I joked feebly to the A&E doctor.

I guess I'll never know exactly what happened when I fell off that youngster, because no one dares tell me. Did the saddle slip? Did I get my foot caught in the stirrup? Had I been dragged? Did my head hit a jump stand? All they would say was that I'd been unconscious for half an hour. Although none of my super-ficial cuts and bruises hurt, I was aware of relentless pins and needles down the right-hand side of my body.

The doctor sent me for X-ray. I asked the technician if he could see any breaks. He said he couldn't and reckoned I might be going home that night. I was doubtful.

"I've broken my neck," I told him. "I can feel it."

Ten minutes later, the doctor came in to confirm my self-diag-nosis. I definitely had fractures in the C3 and C4 vertebrae of my spine. They weren't sure then about C5. Something was showing but it wasn't clear, because of distension and swelling, whether this was a fresh fracture or an old injury. So there it was. I'd told them I knew my neck was broken but didn't really take in the full implications at that point.

I wanted Laura to arrive so she could start making phone calls to owners, as well as to Dr Whitehead, the team doctor; Will Connell, World Class Performance Director; and Rob Hoekstra, Team Manager. They would know what to do. They would know the best people to help fix me. After all, the Olympics were only nine months away.

When Laura arrived a couple of hours later, she was very calm about everything. It turned out that she thought she was coming to pick me up. She had spoken to the guy who had come with me in the ambulance and he'd been told that they'd seen nothing serious on the X-ray. Laura was pretty used to seeing me covered in cuts and bruises so she was relaxed. Until, that is, she asked when we could leave for home.

"You're not taking him anywhere: he's broken his neck in two, or possibly three, places," the medics told her.

I'm sure she would have loved to have sworn or even burst into tears but she refused to show any panic in front of me. Calmly, she asked me for my phone as there were a few calls she had to make. One of them was to the girls on the yard at home – it was Joseph's birthday the next morning and she had to make sure things were organised for the occasion.

It was then that the gravity of the situation hit me like a kick in the gut. I felt the panic rising and tried taking deep breaths to control my fear, but it hurt when I did. So I fixed my eyes on the ceiling and told myself, again and again, I would be okay. Laura left to make calls, leaving me alone with the doctor.

Stupid as it may sound now, I remember saying to him that I'd been to the last Olympic Games and I wanted to go to the next Olympics in London, so he mustn't think he was dealing with just anybody. I guess it was the fear talking and I'm so embarrassed about it now. Medical professionals treat everyone the same – a broken neck is a broken neck – but I so wanted them to understand my dilemma. It still makes me cringe now to think about that outburst but, when you're scared and confused, you cling on to anything that might save you.

They put me in a different collar and took me to a small observation room. I was strapped to the bed that night and couldn't get comfy enough to sleep. All I remember was the pain, the unbelievable pain. For whatever reason, the only way I could get any relief was to put my fists under my backside to lift it up. The nurses went mental, instructing me to keep absolutely still. I had tubes going in and coming out of me, with monitors all around. It must have looked as if I was at death's door. I overheard the nurses talking about neurological damage – paralysis. This was the first time I'd heard them use that word, as they'd been careful not to say it until now. I was terrified.

Apparently, I was suffering some sort of internal shutdown. This happens sometimes when the body goes into shock, causing all kinds of problems. Organs stop working so you have to be very carefully monitored. The doctors at Shrewsbury wanted to move me to the specialist Midlands Spinal Unit in Oswestry, just 20 minutes up the road. I spent one more night at Shrewsbury and then the dreaded spinal board came out in preparation for the transfer. Just the thought of it made my blood pressure go through the roof. I made a point of telling the paramedics that if they strapped me in too tight, I'd freak out. But they were brilliant and I barely remember the move.

On arrival at Oswestry, I was put in a bed close to the nurses' station. Every time they walked past, I kept asking if I was going to be all right. They'd just say, "Let's hope so." I didn't feel blessed with much hope right then. In fact, everyone was emphasising the word 'hope' and every time they did, I sunk a little lower. Hope isn't something I'd ever relied on. I'm a doer – I set targets and I strive to achieve them. I don't just sit back and hope for the best.

Escaping into sleep wasn't even possible, because of the pain. The medical staff would come into my room every four hours to stick pins into my legs and feet, or touch them with blunt or sharp instruments. My plastic neck collar really cut into me. One night, I tried to rip it off because it was hurting so badly. I had a real panic attack. I shouldn't have done that, of course, but it was making me red raw. I'd be restless at night, unable to sleep. I don't know what it is about hospitals, but they're always warm and this one was no exception. It was really, unbearably hot. Perspiration was pouring off me, soaking the sheets and making me itchy and sore.

I was pretty spaced out with painkillers and sleeping pills, but I soon woke up when it came to undergoing CAT scans. Irrationally, they brought on the same suffocating effects as being strapped to the spinal board. I discovered that I was slightly claustrophobic. Those 30 minutes in the scanner seemed like an eternity and I had a couple of rocky moments when I thought I was going to lose it completely. As my heart would start to pound, the technician's voice would come over the intercom: "Not long now, Tim, just hold as still as you can for me." I was a quivering wreck when they finally pulled me out.

The MRI and CAT scans showed three fractures, not that it mattered how many I had to the doctors. A fracture is a fracture and I was going nowhere until they'd healed. So how would my story play out? For large chunks of time, I sunk back into my pit of despair, looking back at my life as if it was ending. Every time a doctor came in, I asked the same question: "Could I be ready for the Olympics?" I'm sure they got sick of it but just humoured me with encouraging replies. It would take time before they'd be able to see how the fractures were healing and give a considered outcome. No one even mentioned riding. As far as they were concerned, I was lucky to be alive, and they told me this regularly.

I cannot tell you how disconcerting it is to hear people around you but not be able to see them because all you can see is the ceiling. Lisa, my sister-in-law, brought me some prism glasses which she'd found on the Internet. Imagine having your Christmas and birthday all rolled into one – that's how I felt when given these glasses. They were a revelation. Obviously, I spent my whole time looking at the ceiling but, when I put these specs on, I could see what was at my feet because of a clever mirror system. I used to balance them on my head, so that I could see when someone walked into the room.

With my glasses, I could see Paul my room-mate. All told, we spent three weeks living together in the same ward, just about 20 feet apart, although we didn't converse very much. It was usually just, "Morning, Paul." "Morning, Tim." There were even days when we didn't speak at all, often because one, or both of us was either plugged into earphones or gazing at the ceiling. While Paul had been the model patient, I'd been an absolute pain in the backside. The naggings and rollicking I got for trying to move when I needed to stay immobile were endless. I can't even sit still by a pool on holiday, so how was I meant to lie motionless in bed for weeks? I wasn't a very good patient and I know I drove everyone crazy in Wrekin Ward.

I can't really remember the kids coming to see me in the beginning. Laura told me later they were worried about seeing me, thinking I'd be wired up to all sorts of machines. When they did come to Oswestry, Laura said they both got to the door and just stood there transfixed. She had to coax them inside and assure them I was all right. I heard her say: "Hello, Daddy." She almost had to push them over to me. Every visit gradually became easier for them though; and by the end they were climbing onto the bed with me. With each visit, Laura brought up more and more emails, letters and cards which we pinned to the board behind my bed. Although I couldn't see them from my position, everyone who came in would read and re-read them to me. Many were from friends but most were from keen show-jumping supporters wishing me a swift recovery.

They were wonderful and really helped to get me through. I had an amazing amount of visitors, too. I'm sure a lot of them wondered why they'd come when I was at my lowest. I might not have said much, but getting news about shows and the sport, in general, was a real pick-me-up. Horse breeder Charlie Edwards came to see me twice a week, always bringing cake or biscuits. He'd just chat away and tell stories that made me smile. Geoff Billington was also a frequent visitor. He'd come into the ward straight from the yard, in his riding clothes – boots, spurs and all. The strangest looking Florence Nightingale you'll ever see.

I remember saying to Laura one day very early on: "I don't think I can do this. I just don't think I can do it." Laura isn't a soft touch for sympathy – she's seen me in plenty of scrapes. "You've no choice. You're doing it and you'll do as you're told," she said firmly.

Throughout this experience – my accident and recovery – Laura remained so strong for me and all of us. So many people have commented on the amazing strength of character she has, how good she is in a crisis. I don't think I really appreciated it at the time but, looking back, I can see it now. That's just who she is. I also know for a fact, because people have told me, that she really did struggle with everything that happened and had some particularly dark moments. But being the kind of person she is, she was able to hold it together in front of me and the kids, because she could see how fragile I was. I hope she knows that I wouldn't have got through this without her. I don't know if I ever told her that, but it's true.

Chapter 28

A new beginning

- Coping in hospital
- Back on a horse
- Competing again
- A change of priorities

Mr Osman, my consultant, came by to see me every day; he kept the conversations brief, avoiding the subject about me riding again. He finally gave me the good news that the spinal cord wasn't permanently damaged and the rest of the spine would all heal well, providing I didn't move. He reminded me that nerves take time to heal, as do bones, and the broken ones in my neck were far from mended. I would have to remain still for a few weeks longer until they were happy that both had repaired enough for me to begin rehabilitation – a few weeks, probably followed by months of physiotherapy. The light that had appeared at the end of my miserable little tunnel suddenly got dimmer again, but at least the light was there and that was all I needed, the briefest of sparks to get me planning again. Give me a target and I'll get there, by hook or by crook.

Mr El Masri, Honorary Clinical Professor, used to come and visit me during his rounds although I wasn't on his list. It was nice of him to take time to see me and this reassured me that everything would be okay. He must have thought I was completely bonkers when all I talked about was getting back in the saddle. Most people would be happy to know that they were going to be walking out of hospital in six weeks without any permanent problems. That wasn't enough for me, I needed to know that I'd be ready for London 2012 and I needed dates. I've always liked to be able to plan my fitness routine with my horses. Why would I be any different?

Every day someone would come round with the excruciating blood-thinning injections they put in my stomach. I was told they were essential when I complained that they were just doing it to torture me. I'm sure they all got fed up with my jokes and quips. I still had mild pins and needles but the feeling had returned to my right-hand side and the pain had gone. Most of the bruising had started to fade. I couldn't wait to escape.

Laura had managed to drive into a wall of the house – her foot slipped off the pedal while she was parking and she was dreading the moment she had to tell me. In fact, she put it off for two visits. I just wanted to get home. I knew that I couldn't just get up and walk out, the risk was too high. I'd lie in bed doing little exercises, making sure I kept my strength up. I remembered too well my broken knee and after only three weeks in plaster, my leg was as weak as a kitten's.

After another scan, it was decided that I'd be strong enough to have some physiotherapy. I'd have weights attached to my ankles and I'd have to lift them slowly and not too high.

"Just do 10 on each leg and I'll come back," said the therapist as she went off to answer the phone.

She came back 20 minutes later and I was still at it. "What are you doing? You'll be exhausted!" I'd have kept going all day if it would have got me out any sooner.

Paul, my room-mate was a couple of weeks ahead of me on his bed rest so when he got his good news that he'd be able to start getting ready to go home, I thought I'd watch carefully so I'd be prepared for what was in store. They started sitting him up in bed in preparation for standing him up on his feet.

The next day, they put his bed up by 30 degrees but Paul complained of headaches and nausea. I could hear all the commotion in his bay opposite me and it sounded as if the man was being tortured. I couldn't see what was happening but it had taken all day, inch by painful inch, to get him up. The muscles had deteriorated so much, I was horrified.

If lying helpless for five weeks wasn't undignified enough, I'd be going through the same humiliating process soon. So I made a pledge that that night, I would start to try and sit up in bed without the nurses knowing – crazy really, considering my state of health, but I had to start taking control of my body. Besides, it gave me something to focus my mind. I hatched a plot to time my secret exercises so that the nurses wouldn't catch me. I was like a naughty child.

The nurses would do a final ward round at 11.30pm and we were at the end of their rounds, so that night, I asked the duty nurse if she would draw the curtains around my bed because I wanted to read and didn't want to disturb Paul. As soon as I heard her footsteps disappear down the corridor, I started the exercise routine I'd planned in my head – slowly trying to sit up, very carefully, holding the side of the bed so I didn't wobble off. The thought of falling out of bed almost made me laugh. Can you imagine what the nurses would have said if they'd found me on the floor?

The next day, I was exhausted from my nocturnal escapades. The nurses came and sat Paul up again, setting the routine for the next couple of days until it was finally time for him to stand. But when the time eventually came for him to get on his feet, he just sank back down to the bed because his leg muscles couldn't hold him up. This was my first glimpse of Paul. He was a young man and not weak by any means.

That night, instead of just sitting up in bed which I was now doing on a regular basis, I'd let my legs hang over the side of the bed and I'd read. This continued for a few more nights until I felt ready to see if I could stand up for my own peace of mind. I put my feet on the floor and sat there for a while. It felt so good.

The only person I told about my nightly escapades was Ivan: "You silly sod. Be careful!" was all he said. I think he knew there'd be no stopping me. I was so happy on my feet, I knew it was wrong and I was being a fool but I couldn't help myself. The gravity of what I was doing never really occurred to me, I was so focused on the immediate benefits that I never thought about the risk I was taking – one slip and I could have done unimaginable damage.

The following week, I was told that the plan was to sit me up – you should have seen their faces when I walked the same day, it was perfect, as if they'd witnessed a miracle – I call it my Lazarus moment. It normally took much longer to get patients back on their feet but because I'd been cheating, I got a head start. Besides, Laura had been telling people that they were going to stand me up that week, so I wanted to put on a decent show. I didn't tell them what I'd been doing, but I think they probably guessed.

If I could walk, then I was determined to get started on my physical therapy, so I threw myself into the rehabilitation, even though I was only allowed to exercise for a short period each day. I had to be careful and I was frequently told that I mustn't push myself too hard. It was disturbing having a body that was so weak.

I had managed to maintain enough muscle and cardiovascular tone not to faint when I first stood up, but other than a stroll around my hospital bed, I hadn't had any exercise in five-and-a-half weeks. It's amazing how quickly you go to seed. I don't think I had ever been so unfit in my life. My joints felt stiff and unwilling, and my tendons and ligaments complained when put under any form of strain. However, my old knee injury proved to be the most troublesome niggle for me, as it made my leg feel rigid and immobile.

I was sent home a few days later still in my collar, feeling fragile. We hadn't told the children I was going to be coming home, as I wanted it to be a surprise. I stood in the hallway tucked around the corner as they walked in from school. I just stood quietly there in the shadows. Mark looked straight at me for a second and then away, then all of a sudden ran into my arms. In that first glance, it hadn't registered.

"I thought you were Uncle Ivan, then I saw your necklace!" he said. I loved that name for it, much better than collar. I had my hair cut that night when I got home. We took the collar off for a few minutes so it didn't get hairy. It felt like my head would fall off and my neck was so weak that I had to hold my head with my hands.

I was told to take it easy, but that's not my style. I went for frequent walks around the yard but didn't get far before I felt tired. I'd set myself targets working backwards from London 2012. I knew that Frankie needed to be ready for Royal Windsor and in order to get him there, I'd need to be riding and jumping by March. That seemed realistic to me but not everyone else around me. Mr Osman didn't want me on a horse till he'd seen me again in February. That would only give me three weeks. To get on a horse ready to jump at a decent level is tough enough, let alone me being ready in that time – it would be impossible.

We'd been planning to still go to Olympia because Mark was taking part in the finale. I was a bit worried about going, because I felt very fragile and also because of my collar – I stuck out like a sore thumb. As it turned out, I ended up doing a stint on TV with Clare Balding for the BBC. Poor Jennifer Saunders met me there, all wrapped up in my neck brace, and was told I'd be giving her training for a programme she was planning in the spring. She must have wondered if getting back into jumping was a good idea seeing me.

A week after having my collar off, in mid-January 2012, I sat on a horse for the first time in three months. I didn't tell Mr Osman or Mr El Masri of course. I had been told that I needed to regain my muscle strength without the collar for support. They wanted to make sure things were healing properly and that the muscles were strong enough to prevent whiplash, but I couldn't wait any longer. I had been having regular physiotherapy from Andy Thomas, our Team GBR physiotherapist and he was happy with things, which was good enough for me.

I didn't feel nervous about getting on Frankie – I chose him as the first horse because he is so laid-back. Once I was on, I realised how ineffective my riding muscles were. I was completely out of shape and no amount of gym work could target them. It was very frustrating at first but it didn't take long for my muscles to remember their job.

I went to a few low-profile shows in April before setting my sights on Royal Windsor as my first major competition. I was a little nervous before the show, I'll be honest, as I knew that everyone would be watching me closely, looking for signs that I wasn't 100% fit after I'd made such a swift comeback. The show couldn't have gone any better really. Frankie was second in the Grand Prix and Fresh Direct K2 (Big), owned by John and Janet Cosgrove, won the Six Bar Challenge.

There was a hairy moment, though, when I fell off after the finish line in the last round of the Six Bar. Big tried really hard over the last fence which was two metres tall, but he twisted slightly in the air and I was shot out the side door. As I was falling through the air, all I thought was, 'Tuck and roll'. It was the first time I'd hit the deck since that fateful day in Wales. I heard the gasp of the crowd, who probably thought my head might fall off, and then the silence as they waited to see if I was okay. I stuck my thumb up to them to signal I was all right and they let out a huge cheer. My neck was pretty sore the next day but it served to show that I wasn't made of china, and it was good to get that first fall out of the way.

Although I still didn't feel entirely comfortable back in the saddle, my results at Royal Windsor gave me a much-needed confidence boost. I knew that Olympic selection for me depended as much on the performances of the other hopefuls as it did on my own performance. I'd pushed myself really hard after the fall and knew I had little time to impress Rob Hoekstra.

I was selected to jump on the Nations Cup Team in St Gallen, Switzerland, at the beginning of June and if I had any chance of being considered for a place on the Olympic squad, I had to go well there. The pressure was on; we rose to the challenge and jumped the only double clear for Great Britain that weekend in the Nations Cup. But to top it off, we also went into the lead in the Grand Prix, only just being beaten into second place by Marcus Ehning. I could see Greenwich Park in my sights and I couldn't have asked for more. On that result, Rob selected me for Rotterdam at the end of June.

As much as we tried our best in Rotterdam, things didn't exactly go to plan for me and Frankie and it wasn't to be. I was asked to go first, a position I don't normally mind but that day there was a lot of pressure, everyone was fighting for a place on the Olympic Team. For a number of reasons things didn't go the way I'd hoped. I knew immediately that we wouldn't be going to London. To all intents and purposes, I was gutted, absolutely devastated for a long time after Rotterdam. I knew I had blown it. Everything I had been working for since my comeback had been in vain and I felt entirely deflated and exhausted. What made it worse was that I had come so close, in real contention of getting a place.

The London Olympic Games were absolutely amazing in every way; I would obviously have loved to have been a part of that. The equestrian teams were incredible to watch and I really enjoyed my trips to London to see it all happen. Our family trip to the Olympic Village was something we'll never forget. One thing is for sure, though, I am planning to be part of the next one in Rio. I'm not finished yet.

I'm a doer, and if I want something I go out and get it. I won't let anything stand in my way. "You make your own luck," someone once said to me and it's true. You can't stand still and wait for things to be handed to you on a plate. It won't happen, you have to work hard and push yourself. Sometimes you're lucky in life, sometimes you're not; you just have to play to your strengths.

I have in my yard the most beautiful young horse who I think has the potential to make it to the top. The Toymaker (given that name by Mark because I go out to shows to win money to buy him toys) is my 'handwriting' as we say in the sport and I loved him from the moment I sat on him. He is owned by Marjorie Glasgow and Laura. Olympic selection in 2016? I hope so.

The immediate future lies with my boys – they love doing so many different things. So whether they want to play rugby, cricket or the drums, or become riders, I don't mind. Whatever they choose to do in life, I will make sure they stick by my work ethic. Whatever knocks you take, physical or otherwise, you have to pick yourself up and brush yourself down and remember… "There's no such word as can't – you will or you won't!"

Acknowledgments

Writing this book has given me an opportunity to recognise and thank so many people who've had a huge impact on my life. Each one of them has been instrumental in making my career happen. Without them, I probably wouldn't be doing what I am today. First and foremost, my thanks go to my parents – to Dad, for buying us our ponies; and Mum, for sending me to riding school in the first place (albeit against my will).

Thanks also go to showjumpers, Mike Saywell and Graham Fletcher, who believed in me and unselfishly encouraged me up the showjumping ladder. I am indebted to all my owners, past and present, who have had similar faith in me. Together, we have shared the many highs and occasional lows of this amazing sport.

In particular, my gratitude extends to friends and owners, John and Janet Cosgrove, for their continued support and advice; and for being there when I need guidance.

Much appreciation also goes to other loyal owners: Lutz Meyerding; Sue Ricketts; Catherine O'Neill; Sue Chubb; Gail McBride; Kevin and Jeanette Edwards; John and Sue Bosher; Colin and Ann Garratt; Derek and Jenny Ward; and Marjorie Glasgow.

Of course, huge thanks go to the backstage crew of friends and staff, including my grooms, physios, farriers and vets – especially Thorsten Feddern – for all the support they have given to keep this show on the road.

I'm immensely grateful to each of my sponsors over the years for their valued help and support. They've all been great, but I must give special mention to Les and Fay Harris of Fresh Direct.

Needless to say, I extend heartfelt thanks to the dedicated team at the Midland Spinal Injuries Unit, Oswestry, who kept my spirits up and nursed me back to health, after my accident at the end of 2011. I cannot praise them enough, not only for truly outstanding medical care, but also for sheer patience in putting up with me.

Finally, thanks go to my family for being constantly alongside me on this rollercoaster ride. To coin a somewhat clichéd phrase that's nevertheless true: None of this would have been possible without you – any of you.

Index

Index

H

I

J

K

L

W

Wade, Alastair (Wadey)
40, 41
Wade, Tony 98
Wales and West Horse Show
157
Ward, Jenny 196
Wax, Ruby 196, 198, 199
Welham 25
Wellow Park Stables 14
Whitaker, Ellen 204
Whitaker, John 37, 91, 103,
109, 167-169, 204, 207
Whitaker, Michael 37, 91, 99,
109, 167, 204, 207
Whitehead, Dr Peter 5, 216
Wilcox, Ann 48, 50
Wilcox, Chris 48, 50
Willetts, Margaret 14, 18
Wiston Bridget 158, 161-163,
165, 167, 168, 171, 181-183
Woody (see Glenwood
Springs)
Wordley, Sharn 157

Z

Zilli, Aldo 50